# REMEMBRANCE OF OUR ANCESTORS
## IN THE FAITH

Now will I praise those godly men [and women],
 our ancestors, each in his [or her] own time:
The abounding glory of the Most High's portion,
 his own part, since the days of old.

Subduers of the land in kingly fashion,
 men of renown for their might,
Or counselors in their prudence,
 or seers of all things in prophecy;

Resolute princes of the folk,
 and governors with their staves;
Authors skilled in composition,
 and forgers of epigrams with their spikes;

Composers of melodious psalms,
 or discoursers on lyric themes;
Stalwart men [and women], solidly established
 and at peace in their own estates—
All these were glorious in their time,
 each illustrious in his [or her] day.

Their wealth remains in their families,
 their heritage with their descendants;
Through God's covenant with them their family endures,
 their posterity for their sake.

And for all time their progeny will endure,
 their glory will never be blotted out;
Their bodies are peacefully laid away,
 but their name lives on and on.
At gatherings their wisdom is retold,
 and the assembly proclaims their praise.

*(Sirach 44:1-7, 11-15)*

# GREAT PEOPLE
## of the
## BIBLE

# Great People of the Bible

---

## LIVING PORTRAITS
## IN WORD AND PICTURE

By
REV. JUDE WINKLER, OFM, CONV.

---

ILLUSTRATED IN FULL COLOR

CATHOLIC BOOK PUBLISHING CO.
New York

IMPRIMI POTEST: Daniel Pietrzak, OFM, CONV.
*Minister Provincial of St. Anthony of Padua Province (USA)*

NIHIL OBSTAT: Daniel V. Flynn, J.C.D.
*Censor Librorum*

IMPRIMATUR: ✠ Joseph T. O'Keefe, D.D.
*Vicar General, Archdiocese of New York*

The Nihil obstat and imprimatur are official declarations that a book or pamphlet is free of doctrinal or moral error. No implication is contained therein that those who have granted the nihil obstat and imprimatur agree with the contents, opinions or statements expressed.

## DEDICATION

To my parents, whose love has guided me
and
To the Knoorens, in whose house I first read about these people.

(T-485)

# Introduction

A FEW years ago while I was stationed in Rome to complete my studies, one of the friars told me about something that had happened in his catechism class.

The fall before there had been a TV special about Moses and now, being Easter time, *Jesus of Nazareth* by Zefferrelli was being broadcast. This friar's class was discussing the program, and one of the students asked him whether we should believe that Jesus really existed or whether it was like the things that they had showed about Moses. In saying that, she gave the Italian hand gesture that made it obvious she didn't put much credence in any of it.

This type of attitude is not very uncommon today. We live in a TV age. Every evening we hear about people and their problems. We share an hour with these TV people, and then we shelve them for another week. We know that they are not real and that we can turn them on and off at will.

This sort of activity eventually produces a TV mentality that goes beyond what we are watching on TV. Many people now treat God as if He were a TV personality. They turn Him on for 45 minutes every Sunday morning, but He is ignored the rest of the week.

If that is true of God, it is all the more true of people who are found in the Bible. We put King David, for example, on the same level as we might a favorite soap opera character. Both are nice, but they don't have anything to do with our real lives.

This book is written to show that the figures in the Bible are real people. They lived and breathed, they sinned and sought forgiveness, and they struggled to believe even as we do today.

Most of all, these people of the Bible can and must speak to us. They are not fantasies—they are our ancestors in faith. When we read about them, we should have the same feeling that we receive when we look at an old family album.

When we page through that album, we want to see what our ancestors looked like, and we ask what they were like in character and temperament. We soak up any information about them that we can receive because they are our flesh and blood. How much more should we be interested in our family in faith?

The present book can provide helpful insights into the major biblical figures treated—especially through the magnificent full color illustrations that graphically portray some of the salient traits of the subjects—and fix them deep in one's imagination.

The editors and I hope that this book will stimulate people's interest and make them want to read and study the Bible.

# Contents

# THE NEW TESTAMENT

# THE
# OLD TESTAMENT

# Adam  The First Man

*Genesis 1—5*

WHEN we think back to reflect upon our ancestors, a certain pattern usually develops. For the first few generations we know numerous details about them—names, dates, places. As the clock goes back, however, we slowly lose details.

Eventually we are left with nothing more than a name by which we can remember them, and then we pass to the time when even names are lost.

The authors of the court of Kings David and Solomon (called the Yahwist school of writing) faced a similar development when they wrote about how God had guided Israel. For the first few generations, they had many details, but as they went farther back, the details evaporated.

These sacred writers wanted to state that they firmly believed God had guided their ancestors always, even from the first days of creation. However, they faced the practical difficulty of having so little information with which they could work. They didn't even have a name to assign to the first man or woman.

It was for that reason that these authors searched the pagan myths of their days for elements that they might borrow for their account of creation. They borrowed selectively, though, carefully removing anything that was blatantly pagan.

Their account (Genesis 2) made it very clear that they believed that God created the first man and woman. They gave that first man a generic name, Adam, for that name in Hebrew means nothing more than "man." (That name also has a certain word-play with the Hebrew word "Adamah" which means dirt, for God created man by giving his spirit into a mound of lifeless dirt.)

Around 400 years after this first account had been written, another school of authors, the Priestly authors, wrote their own account of creation (Genesis 1) to complete the first account. In this account creation is spread out over a seven-day period.

This Priestly account is even more anti-pagan than the older account in chapter 2, for it makes clear that all creation depends upon God for its existence (and is thus not equal in power to God).

The Yahwist authors completed their account of Adam's creation by speaking about his rapport with God. Adam destroyed the friendship that God had intended by disobeying God's command about the fruit of the tree in the garden.

God had told him not to eat of it, but Adam, anxious to prove his independence and dissatisfied with his having to listen to God, ate of it anyway.

The story still speaks to us today. So often we want to be more important or rich or intelligent than we are instead of accepting what God has given us—and this is the same sin as that of Adam.

# Eve   The Mother of All the Living

*Genesis 1—4*

HER name is an indication of her somewhat ambiguous status in the history of humankind. She is called Eve, a name that has two possible meanings. The more commonly accepted meaning for her name is "living," for she is the mother of all who live.

There is another meaning for her name, though, which alludes to her more negative role in history. In some oriental languages her name could mean serpent, a reminder that she and the serpent brought death into the world.

In the Priestly account of creation in chapter one of Genesis, woman is created at the same time as man. She is his equal. This is not true of the Yahwist account in chapter two, for in it she is created after man and is obviously subservient to him.

In the Yahwist account, God decided that man needed a companion. He first created animals, but they were not suitable. He then took a rib from man and formed Eve. She was his perfect companion, and together they were humankind.

Even here, though, the rabbis speak of how her role was ambiguous. Playing with words a bit, they say that she was created as a "helpmate against man." Created to help him, she often turned against him. (It is obvious that these opinions originated in a male dominated society.)

It is in chapter three that the story of the first man and woman becomes tragic. God had ordered them not to eat of the fruit of one of the trees in the garden. One day the serpent enticed Eve. He told her that God had ordered them not to eat of the fruit because He was jealous of them.

Eve fell for his trick, and she ate the fruit and then gave some of it to her husband. There is a terrible irony here. She had been created to be one with man, and now she was hurting him in a horrendous manner.

God punished the man, woman, and serpent for their sin. Speaking to the woman, He condemned her to suffer the pains of childbirth. It also seems as if He condemned her to long for her husband but never to be truly satisfied.

With both of these penalties, the author is reflecting on what he saw in his own times. He couldn't believe that God created things the way they were now, so they must have become that way because sin had entered the world.

The stories of Adam and Eve remind us that the first Adam brought sin into the world and the second, Jesus, brought life. Likewise the first woman, Eve, brought death and division into the world through her sin while the second Eve, Mary, the mother of Jesus, brought life through her obedience to the call of God.

# Cain and Abel   The First Murder

*Genesis 4*

THERE is possibly no greater tragedy than when a family breaks apart in violence. The bonds of blood should bind brothers and sisters to one another, but sometimes deep divisions develop that can have disastrous consequences.

All who see what is happening know that there is something very wrong taking place—something that goes against the very nature of things—but they are often powerless to stop it.

The Yahwist authors who wrote the story of Cain and Abel recognized the wrongness in fraternal violence. It so shocked them that they decided to use the story of a fratricide as an example of how society could quickly and disastrously degenerate after sin had entered the world.

God had created humankind to be good, but once Adam and Eve sinned, there was nothing holding them back from careening into this deplorable state in which even the most sacred of bonds were treated with no respect.

Cain and Abel were the first of Adam and Eve's children. They each chose a different occupation—Cain was a farmer and Abel a shepherd.

One day each of the brothers decided to make an offering to the Lord. The Lord accepted Abel's offering, but He did not accept Cain's.

At this point we must be careful not to read too much into the story, for it never explains why God didn't accept Cain's offering (we really don't know if his offering was of inferior quality or not).

Cain became disturbed by what had happened. Seeing this, God warned him that he was endangering himself by risking sin. (We can see God's love and concern for Cain in this warning.) Cain ignored the advice and took his brother out into a field where he killed him.

Nature rebelled at this horrendous act, and the earth cried out to God for justice. Cain denied knowing what had become of his brother, even denying any responsibility for his brother's safety.

Because of Cain's crime, God punished him by decreeing that he would become a nomad on the earth. He did show His love for Cain once again, though, by marking him with a sign that would protect him from all those who might wish to kill him.

The story is filled with lessons. First among them is the effect of sin upon humanity (how animal-like human beings become). There is also the lesson of responsibility toward one's brothers and sisters (all of humanity).

Another important lesson is that which Cain should have learned—God loves each of us in His own particular way. We should not be jealous of the way He loves others, but rather rejoice in His love for us.

# Noah   And the Flood

*Genesis 6—10*

NO matter how much patience one has, a moment arrives when a person concludes that things must change. The only possibility left open is to take some form of drastic action.

This is the impression we receive upon reading the first chapters of the book of Genesis. Once Adam and Eve had sinned, things rapidly became worse and worse. Humankind degenerated until people were beastlike. God, who had created human beings to be good, was bitterly disappointed at this turn of events.

God decided that the only way to deal with the problem was to annihilate what He had created and to begin all over again from scratch. To do this, He chose one good man, Noah, and told him to build an ark. He was to take his family into the ark along with all different types of animals. Once they were safely inside the ark, God opened the floodgates of heaven and allowed the whole world to be inundated.

After forty days of rain, the Lord once again closed the floodgates of heaven. Slowly the earth dried up, and when dry land appeared, Noah and his family descended from the ark. They gave thanks to God for their deliverance and presented a sacrificial offering to him.

God was gratified at the show of gratitude on the part of humans (as opposed to the rampant disobedience before the flood). He promised humankind that He would never again destroy the earth by flood, and as a sign of His pledge He placed the rainbow in the sky.

This is the first of the covenants (or pacts) reported in the Bible. Gradually God would bind Himself closer and closer to humankind by these covenants until He would become one with us in the new covenant, Jesus.

The story of Noah, like the stories of most of the first eleven chapters of Genesis, should not be accepted too historically. The authors of these chapters wanted to present lessons rather than biographies, and to do that they borrowed some details from pagan myths.

Noah's story, for example, bears striking similarity to the Mesopotamian story, "Gilgamesh." Some scholars have said that Noah was nothing other than a cheap plagiarism of Gilgamesh. That evaluation is unfair, though, for there are also major differences between the two accounts.

Although the biblical authors began with the Gilgamesh story, they changed the details of the story in a striking manner. One of the most important of their changes is the attitude of God during the flood. The Mesopotamian gods never show love—they are selfish and capricious. The God of the Israelites is a God who loves and who even binds Himself to a covenant—a promise that was fulfilled only in the birth and death of Jesus.

# Abraham     Man of Faith

*Genesis 11:27—25:11; Romans 4:1ff; Galatians 3:6ff*

ABRAHAM, the first of the patriarchs, is also known as the father of faith (as well as being the father of both the Jewish and the Arab peoples). His story can be found in the book of Genesis beginning with chapter 12.

In the earlier chapters of Genesis, God had addressed His call to all of humanity, but over and over again they rejected His call by sinning. God thus decided to change tactics; so He called one man through whom He would save all: Abraham, the son of Terah from the city of Ur.

Abraham is the Father of Faith because his rapport with God was one of total trust in the will of God. When God first called him, he left everything—his land, kinsmen, his goods—and traveled to the land to which God directed him. God, on His part, promised that Abraham would inherit that land and become a great man.

Yet, Abraham's faith was often tried. He faced famine, dangers from foreign kings, and battles to protect his family. The greatest challenge to Abraham's faith, though, involved the covenant that God had made with him.

A covenant is a treaty used in ancient times in which two parties bind themselves to certain obligations toward each other. The covenant into which God entered with Abraham is described in chapters 15 and 18. God greatly humbled Himself by entering into this covenant, for He bound himself to do certain things for Abraham but He did not require anything of Abraham.

God promised Abraham that in addition to becoming great and possessing the land, he would also become the father of many descendents. They, in fact, would be more numerous than the stars of the heavens.

God was painfully slow in fulfilling these promises. Although Abraham was promised possession of the land, he only owned a small grave plot at his death. He did become a rich man, but for most of his life he was childless, for Sarah, his wife, was barren.

Sarah sent her servant in to Abraham so that she might have a child through adoption (this was the practice of those days), and her servant Hagar bore a son, Ishmael. When Sarah's own son, Isaac, was born, God ordered that Ishmael be expelled. Abraham, a man of faith, obeyed the Lord.

Then the Lord ordered that Isaac, the only remaining heir, be sacrificed. Again, Abraham gathered the courage to fulfill the will of God.

However, just before Abraham sacrificed his son, an angel of the Lord stopped him. God had sorely tested Abraham, but Abraham had remained totally faithful to God.

Thus, it is not surprising that St. Paul considered Abraham to be the father of all who placed their faith in God.

# Sarah   The Mother of Israel

*Genesis 11—24*

IT is difficult to classify Sarah in any neat pattern, for she is quite different from the other wives of the patriarchs of Israel. Most of the women in the Bible are stereotypes—mere caricatures of people.

Sarah, on the other hand, receives quite a bit of notice. Sarah is not a backdrop against which a story is told. She is a real person whose personality leaps out of the account of the patriarch Abraham. She is the Matriarch of the Jewish people.

Sarah was the half sister of Abraham. (In the days of the patriarchs such weddings were common, especially in Egypt.) Her name was Sarai, a name that was changed to Sarah when Abram's name was changed by God to Abraham.

Sarah seems to have been a beautiful woman for twice she was placed in danger by her desirability (with Pharaoh and King Abimelech). She was also a strong personality, making decisions and having Abraham follow the course of action that she had decided.

Sarah's story revolves around the fact that she was barren. It was considered to be a terrible curse not to be able to have children. To somewhat remedy the situation, Sarah sent her servant girl, Hagar, into Abraham's tent so that she would have a child.

When the child would be born, Sarah was to adopt it and thus, in a way, have her own child.

However, when the child was born, Hagar lorded it over Sarah that she had borne a child while Sarah was still barren.

God made a promise to Abraham that he would have a numerous descendence, but up to this point Abraham had only Ishmael, Hagar's son. One day God visited Abraham's tent where He promised him that Sarah would bear a son.

Sarah overheard the conversation and began to laugh, incredulous at the promise made for she was long past childbearing years. Even after the promise was made it seemed as if all were lost, for she was almost taken into the harem of Abimelech.

God, however, protected Sarah, and she escaped this danger. She bore a son whom she and her husband called Isaac.

After Isaac was born, Sarah showed her forcefulness and her protectiveness for her son by forcing Abraham to send Hagar and her son away. She was distrustful of Ishmael and wanted her son to be the only heir.

We know little else about Sarah except that when she died Abraham bought a grave site where she was buried—the first fulfillment of the promise that God had made that he would possess the land. Thus, we receive a real portrait of Sarah—showing both strengths and weaknesses. She was a real woman who answered God's call and became the mother of a great people.

# Isaac   The Victim

*Genesis 21—28*

ODDLY enough, the children of famous persons rarely attain the importance that their parents do. Very often they live in the shadow of their parents' glory and never seem able to find themselves.

We get this type of an impression when we read about Isaac, the son of Abraham. Isaac never seems to attain the stature of his father. There are, in fact, only two types of stories about Isaac.

In one set of stories Isaac does heroic things, but they are always things that his father has already done. He never seems to be able to do great things on his own.

The other set of stories is an even stronger indication of Isaac's plight—stories in which he is victimized by circumstances.

The most famous of these stories, of course, is that of how Isaac's father almost sacrificed him to God. Very little is said of Isaac's reaction to being tied up and heaped upon a pile of wood and seeing the knife in his father's hand approach him. To say the least, it must have been traumatic.

When Sarah, his mother, died, Abraham sent his servant to find Isaac a wife. Here we see Isaac as totally passive—waiting at home while his future was being decided for him (even Rebekah was more active in the whole affair). This is in sharp contrast to the story of Jacob, Isaac's son, who searches for his own wife.

A number of stories from Isaac's life follow, and they are almost exact copies of what happened to his father.

Like his father, Isaac lived through a bad famine during which he went to Abimelech's kingdom. Like Abraham, he lied about the identity of his wife. Like Abraham, he eventually made a treaty with Abimelech.

Isaac's tendency to be victimized is seen once again at the end of his life. He was blind and nearing death so he called his eldest son, Esau, and ordered him to prepare him a meal. When he had eaten he would give Esau his blessing.

While Esau was gone, Jacob, at the instigation of his mother, prepared Isaac a meal and disguised himself as Esau. Isaac was tricked into giving Jacob the blessing and not Esau.

It is important to realize, however, that in spite of the fact that Isaac was passive and victimized all his life, he did not fail to do God's will.

God never promised us that we would meet with great success and be famous if we followed Him—He promised us only that we would be loved.

Isaac did not have to be as great as Abraham to remain faithful to God. All God asked of him was that he use the gifts that had been given him (as small as they were) to the best of his ability.

# Rebekah   The Wife of Isaac

*Genesis 24—28*

WE often find it difficult to understand why God chooses certain people to be important while others are left to fulfill less important roles.

Very often the choice that God makes contradicts what we would expect—what even seems just to us. We are left with the mystery that God's ways are not like our ways.

We see this mystery in the story of Rebekah, Isaac's wife.

She had been brought to Isaac by one of Abraham's servants who had been sent to Mesopotamia to fetch a wife for Isaac from among Abraham's kin. She showed herself generous in the way in which she had treated Abraham's servant.

Since Rebekah was a good woman and also related to Abraham, the servant went to her home to arrange her marriage to his master's son. When asked whether she approved of this possibility, she quickly acceded.

It is written that Isaac fell in love with her (something that is not to be taken for granted in Old Testament weddings).

Although she was childless for a while, she eventually bore twin sons: Esau and Jacob.

Even in the womb these two sons battled with each other. The firstborn, Esau, was to be the father of the Edomites while Jacob was to be the father of Israel.

Rebekah became involved in God's choice with her two sons. God had chosen Jacob over Esau. Rebekah, likewise, loved Jacob more than she loved her elder son, Esau. Thus, when Isaac, her husband, was dying, she played a trick on him so that he would give Jacob his final blessing and not Esau.

According to the judgment of the world, the blessing belonged to Esau, but God had chosen Jacob for a special role, and He would let nothing stand in His way.

Humanly speaking, however, Rebekah's favoritism for Jacob would have disastrous effects. Jacob, like his mother, would show undue favoritism for one of his sons, Joseph. That favoritism would eventually lead to Joseph's being sold into slavery by his brothers.

It was only after a long time that his brothers were able to accept the fact that God (as well as their father) had chosen Joseph above them and they would just have to live with God's choices.

Even for us it is often difficult to accept the role that God has given us to live. Yet this is exactly what God asks us to do—to take what He has given us and to do our best with it.

Most of all, He asks us to trust in Him, no matter what.

# Jacob   The Man Who Wrestled with God

*Genesis 25:19—50:13*

THERE are some individuals who always seem to be involved in some scheme. Either they are busy tricking someone or they are busy being tricked. Jacob, the son of Isaac, falls into that pattern.

Jacob's name means, "he will trip by the heel," and it alludes to the fact that he was born grasping the heel of his twin brother, Esau. That grasping nature led him first to buy his brother's birthright for a bowl of lentil stew and then to conspire with his mother to steal the blessing his father had intended for Esau.

Following this deception, Jacob fled to his uncle Laban's house. On the way he dreamt that he saw a ladder going up into heaven with angels ascending and descending. During the vision God promised him a large posterity who would possess the land.

Arriving at Laban's house, Jacob met his future bride, Rachel. He worked for Laban for seven years as her price, but his uncle tricked him on his wedding night when he substituted Leah, Rachel's unattractive older sister, for Rachel.

Jacob then worked another seven years to buy Rachel. Leah, her slave, and Rachel's slave all bore many sons to Jacob, but Rachel bore only one, Joseph.

Deciding to return home, Jacob asked Laban for a portion of the flock, and by using crafty means, he managed to increase his por-

tion. He fled to go home but was stopped by Laban who was angry because someone (Rachel) had stolen his household idols. Not finding them, Laban made a pact with Jacob and allowed him to go.

Jacob knew that upon returning home he would meet Esau, the brother he had defrauded. Jacob sent him gifts to appease his anger. The night before he confronted Esau, he wrestled with "God" who gave him a new name, Israel.

This meeting with God seems to have affected Jacob, for the next day instead of using cunning to escape the consequences, he put himself at Esau's mercy (who forgave him). This was the first time that Jacob relied on love and not on cunning.

Jacob settled in Shechem where his daughter, Dinah, was raped. Jacob's sons avenged her dishonor by killing (by trickery) those responsible. Jacob then moved to Bethel where his wife, Rachel, died giving birth to Benjamin.

The rest of Jacob's story is tied to the story of Joseph, Jacob's beloved son (beloved because he was the son of his beloved wife, Rachel). He flaunted his favoritism toward Joseph and roused the jealousy of Joseph's brothers (with tragic consequences).

Joseph, who was sold into slavery by his brothers, eventually became the vizier of Egypt, saving the whole family in time of famine. Jacob died in Egypt, but his body was buried in the promised land.

# Rachel and Leah

*Genesis 29—35*

WHY do we love one person more than another? Why do we find one person attractive while another is just plain for us? Why do we fall madly in love with one while another never produces sparks?

Although it is impossible to answer these questions, it is nevertheless true that these matters have great importance for us. The matters of the heart can make life wonderful or destroy lives.

The story of Leah and Rachel, two sisters and the two wives of Jacob, illustrates this point. They were the daughters of Laban, Jacob's uncle.

Jacob, like his father Isaac, was to find his wife in his ancestral homeland. He found a beautiful girl, Rachel, at a well and helped her to water her flock. He then followed her home for he wanted to marry her (she was also one of his relatives—in ancient times it was normal to marry one's cousin, and such familial marriages were actually preferred).

Jacob stayed with Laban for a while and worked for him by tending his flocks. After a short time Laban asked Jacob what he could pay him for all the work that he was doing. Jacob responded that he would like to marry Rachel. Laban agreed, but after Jacob had worked for him for seven years, Laban reneged on his promise.

Instead of giving Rachel to Jacob, Laban gave him Leah, Rachel's older sister. Since she was covered with a veil, Jacob did not discover this deception until it was too late.

When Jacob asked Laban why he had done this, Laban only responded that it was not their custom to allow a younger sister to marry before the older sister. After another seven years of service Laban gave Jacob Rachel as well.

Leah and Rachel were quite different. Leah seems to have been unattractive while Rachel was ravishing. Leah was quite docile while Rachel was aggressive (as seen when she robbed her father's idols).

Leah was very fertile while Rachel was all but barren, having only two children and dying while giving birth to the second.

Jacob, for some reason, fell head over heels in love with Rachel while he seems to have had a much more distant rapport with Leah. Possibly this was because Rachel was his first love or because she was more attractive than her sister—we just can't be sure why.

However, Jacob's intense love for one wife over the other had tragic consequences that would only fully come to light in the next generation. The children of these two women and their servants (Joseph and his brothers) would have to struggle with the unequal love that Jacob had given to their mothers and to them. They would only slowly learn to accept this fact and live with it.

# Joseph The Favorite Son

*Genesis 29—50*

WE sometimes picture Bible figures as being perfect from their earliest days. We imagine that they had a special line of communication open with God so that anytime they needed Him He would be there. We wonder why this isn't true of people in our own times.

The story of Joseph and his brothers provides an interesting variation of that pattern. He and his brothers were not perfect beings—if anything they were flawed individuals who grew toward integration.

Throughout their story there are very few direct interventions by God—rather God works through natural events. Joseph and his brothers are real people—people with whom we can identify.

The story revolves around the theme of how one of the brothers was loved in a special way by their father, Jacob, and the difficulties that developed because of it. Joseph was obviously favored by Jacob (and God), and his brothers were jealous of him.

Joseph, for his part, was not very prudent in the way he flaunted his status. His brothers decided to get even for being overlooked, and they sold Joseph into slavery.

Joseph proved to be just as fortunate in slavery as he was in his own household. He was virtuous when his master's wife tried to seduce him (because of which he was thrown into prison).

In prison he quickly rose to a position of responsibility. Then he was called before the Pharaoh to interpret one of his dreams.

Joseph told Pharaoh that Egypt would have seven years of good harvests followed by seven years of famine. Pharaoh named Joseph as his vizier in charge of making preparations for the famine.

When the famine arrived, people of every nation flocked to Egypt to buy grain. Joseph's brothers were among those who came.

Joseph first treated his brothers harshly, holding one of them in prison until they returned with their youngest brother. (They did not know that the vizier to whom they were talking was their brother.) When they returned with the boy, he laid another trap for them, telling them the boy would be his slave.

At this point they responded heroically, offering to be slaves themselves as long as the boy would be set free. Joseph realized how much they had grown. He identified himself and assured his brothers that he forgave them.

The story is one of great human growth. Joseph grew from being a conceited child to being a man who could forgive grave injustice.

His brothers grew from being jealous to being capable of admitting their guilt and being ready to suffer for each other. They were even able to admit and accept the fact that Jacob, their father, loved Joseph more than them.

# Moses   The Liberator

*Exodus, Leviticus, Numbers, and Deuteronomy*

LAWGIVER, prophet, leader, judge, mediator, priest—these are only a few of the titles that could be applied to Moses. He made himself an instrument of the Lord, and through him the Lord accomplished great things.

Moses was one of the Bible figures who were chosen by God from birth. He was saved from the murderous edict of Pharaoh who wanted to kill all male Jewish children. His mother put him in a basket in the Nile, and he was found and adopted by Pharaoh's daughter.

As a man, Moses had to choose between his Egyptian upbringing and his Jewish roots. He killed an Egyptian who was maltreating a Jewish slave and was forced to flee for his life.

In Midian, where Moses was a shepherd for his father-in-law, he encountered God in a burning bush. God commissioned him to liberate His people from their slavery in Egypt. At first Moses hesitated, but God assured him that He would work through him.

When Moses and his brother Aaron went to Pharaoh to ask for the freedom of the Jews, though, Pharaoh refused and made the service of their enslavement harder and harder. God sent a series of plagues against Egypt to force Pharaoh's hand, ending in the death of every firstborn male in the land.

Pharaoh relented and sent the Jews away, but he soon reconsidered and pursued them with his army. God miraculously rescued His people by having them pass through the Reed Sea on dry land while He caused Pharaoh and his army to drown there.

God continued to lead His people through the desert to His holy mountain where He gave Moses the ten commandments—guidelines for His people so that they would not stray from His love. They did, however, stray.

The people constantly bemoaned the sacrifices that they had to make in the desert. They rebelled against God, worshiping a golden calf which they had made. They also publicly doubted God's protection when they approached the promised land.

Each time they rebelled against God, He sent diseases and misfortunes to bring them back to their senses. Each time God punished them, however, Moses would intercede for them.

The Jews remained in the desert for forty years, for God decreed that since this was a rebellious people, none of those who left Egypt (except Joshua and Caleb) would enter the promised land.

Moses was only permitted to glimpse the land from a distance. He died on Mount Nebo where, legend has it, God buried him.

Moses is a tremendous example of a man who, although he considered himself to be weak, allowed God's power to work through him—something we must all do.

# Joshua    Successor of Moses

*Exodus 17:8-16; 24:13; 32:17; 33:11; Numbers 13—14; Joshua*

AT times a person's name can reveal a great deal. "Joshua," for example, means, "Yahweh is salvation." This name illustrates the tremendous faith of Joshua and Israel in Yahweh, especially that Yahweh would give them the land promised them from the days of Abraham.

Joshua began his career of service to the Lord as Moses' lieutenant. He led the Israelite forces into battle against Amalek (the battle in which Israel's forces won as long as Moses' arms were raised).

Joshua also accompanied Moses and the seventy elders to the holy mountain where Moses received the ten commandments.

In Exodus 33:11, we read that Joshua used to accompany Moses into the tent where God used to speak to him. When Moses went to transmit that teaching to the camp, Joshua remained in the tent.

Numbers 13—14 tells us that Moses sent twelve men into the land of Canaan to scout the land. Two of the men whom he sent were Joshua and Caleb. When these men returned, all of them except for Joshua and Caleb reported that the land was inhabited by giants and that it would be impossible for them to take it.

The people were greatly discouraged at this report and begged to return to Egypt. Because of this God punished the people and decreed that, of all of them, only Joshua and Caleb would live to enter the promised land.

After Moses' death, Joshua led Israel into the promised land. Like Moses at the Red Sea, Joshua split the waters of the Jordan before the Israelites. On the other side he had all the Israelite males circumcised as a sign of their belonging to the covenant.

Jericho was the first city that the Israelites conquered. The victory was given them by God who miraculously caused the city walls to crumble after the priest had carried the ark in procession around them for seven days.

Ai was the next city. The Israelites' first attempt to take it failed because of their sin, but when the sin was punished they easily defeated their enemies.

The fear of the Israelites spread so that the inhabitants of one city, Gibeon, sued for peace. All the rest of the Canaanites were quickly defeated before Israel.

After most of the land had been conquered, Joshua organized its division among the tribes, and he then conducted a renewal of the covenant. His death is reported at the end of the book bearing his name.

The book of Joshua is probably an idealized accurate account of the conquest of the land. Most scholars believe that the process was much more gradual than reported there. Thus, it is not so much an historical text as a profession of faith that "Yahweh is salvation."

# Rahab   The Prostitute

*Joshua 2; 6:17ff; Matthew 1:5*

RAHAB was a prostitute, and thus symbolic of everything that was bad with the land into which the Israelites were entering (Canaan). Yet she differed from her compatriots.

Rahab recognized that the hand of God was with the Israelites. When the opportunity presented itself, she declared her loyalty to that God and His people.

By doing this, Rahab changed history's evaluation of her. Far from being a symbol of the sexual depravity of the pagans, she became a symbol of the righteous pagan who searches for the truth and who finds that truth in Yahweh, the God of Israel.

Rahab lived in Jericho, the first city that the Israelites encountered upon crossing over the Jordan. Joshua sent two spies into the city to prepare for that invasion.

Rahab hosted them, and when the king sent for them, she lied to the king's men saying that they had already left. Meanwhile, she hid them upon her roof.

When the king's men left, she told the spies that she had protected them because she knew that the Israelites would conquer her land. Fear of them had fallen upon the Canaanites ever since they had heard what had happened at the Red Sea.

That fear had increased when the Israelites defeated the Amorite kings. She begged them to spare her and her family.

The spies promised that when the Israelites captured the city, they would spare Rahab and all of her family. The sign of their protection would be a scarlet cord tied to the window. All who were inside that house would be spared while all outside would die.

The spies then left and, after three days of hiding, returned safely to their camp where they reported to Joshua.

Joshua had the priests process around the city for seven days. On the seventh day, while they processed and shouted and blew their trumpets, the walls of the city came crashing down. The Israelites quickly entered and took the city.

The Israelites searched for Rahab and led her and her family outside the city. They then killed all in the city, putting it to the torch. From then on Rahab lived with the Israelites.

Rahab's name is also mentioned in Matthew 1:5 when she is called the wife of Salmon, the great-grandmother of King David and an ancestor of Jesus. Her great response of faith to the God of Israel not only led to her salvation but was a step in the coming of the Savior into the world.

Rahab's story is a reminder to us that no matter what we have done or how weak we consider ourselves, we can still return to God and do His will.

# Deborah  The Judge of Israel

*Judges 4—5*

ALTHOUGH stereotypes might be distasteful to us, they were not necessarily so to the authors of the Bible. In certain parts of the Bible, in fact, they were used extensively as a type of shorthand.

Since the roles of society were strictly defined, the authors of the books of the Bible could show that a situation was normal if it corresponded with what one would expect or that a situation was unusual if it did not correspond.

It is important to remember this when one considers the prophetess and judge Deborah. She held a most unusual role in the history of Israel. She is the only female judge mentioned in the book of Judges and one of only a few female prophets throughout the history of Israel.

For an Israelite, the place of the women was in the home. Women were stereotyped as being weak and not very wise.

Given this stereotype, it was extraordinary that Deborah should have held the office that she did. The fact that she did could only be attributed to one thing: the Spirit of the Lord.

God alone could take "a weak and unwise woman" and make her the leader of her people.

This lesson is made all the clearer when one considers her role in the war fought against the Canaanites. The people of Israel were being oppressed by the Canaanites whose forces were led by the General Sisera.

Deborah summoned Barak, a man from Naphtali, to convoke 10,000 men from the northern tribes. However, he hesitated; he did not want to go into battle without Deborah for he knew that she was a woman who possessed the power of the Lord.

Deborah agreed to go into battle with Barak's forces, but she warned him that the Lord would not give him all the glory of a victory during the battle. Some of the glory would be given to a woman who would be the person who killed Sisera.

Everything happened exactly as Deborah had prophesied. Barak's forces defeated the army of the Canaanites, but Sisera, their general, escaped. He fled to the tent of a certain Heber, and there he was killed by Jael who drove a tent peg through his temple.

In writing the story of Deborah, the authors of the book of Judges were amazed at what these two women had done. Truly the power of God had shown through their weakness and had accomplished wonders.

No longer was it important if one were weak or strong. All that was important was that each allowed the power of God to work through him or her.

# Gideon    The Faithful Warrior of God

*Judges 6:11—8:22*

GIDEON, like Deborah, was one of the judges of Israel. His service to Israel and the Lord is a sign that God lifts up the weak and humble and makes them instruments of His power.

Even though the twelve tribes of Israel had occupied large portions of Canaan under Joshua, their hold on the land was not secure. The Canaanites would often attack them, and the Israelites were sorely oppressed by their foes.

During one such invasion (by the Midianites), God called Gideon, a man from the tribe of Manasseh, to be judge over Israel. As judge he was to lead the Israelites into battle in the name of their king, the Lord.

Gideon's first reaction to this call was disbelief. There were stronger men in Israel whom God could have chosen. Yet, God assured Gideon that he was to be an instrument of God's wrath.

His first action was to destroy his father's shrine to Baal (a pagan god). The men of his town were horrified at this sacrilege, but Joash, Gideon's father, rebuked them stating that if Baal were really a god, he could punish Gideon himself.

Gideon then called together the tribes of Israel. To prove his authority, he called upon the Lord to perform a sign before all of Israel. The Lord did this, and all of the warriors of Israel were ready to follow Gideon.

The number of warriors was so great, though, that the Lord was concerned lest the Israelites believe that they had defeated Midian by their own power. The Lord thus ordered that many be sent home, ordering Gideon to take with him only those men who lapped up water like dogs when they took a drink. These men numbered only three hundred.

The Midianites, however, were incredibly numerous. The prospects were bleak, but the Lord was with Gideon. He ordered him to divide the forces into three groups with each man carrying a trumpet and an empty jar with a torch hidden inside.

These men then fell upon the Midianite camp in the middle of the night, blowing the trumpets and breaking the jars. The enemy forces panicked and fled.

Gideon's forces pursued them across the Jordan. Being short on supplies, Gideon asked help from the inhabitants of two local cities, but they rebuffed him. He captured the Midianite kings and killed them, along with thousands of their forces. He then punished the elders of the cities which had refused him assistance.

The elders of Israel were grateful to Gideon for his powerful deeds, and they begged him to be their king. However, Gideon refused, for he recognized that Israel had only one king, the Lord, and He was the true author of his fabulous victory.

# Samson The Nazirite

*Judges 13—16*

SAMSON was a wild beast of a man and it is even difficult to see how he could be called a man of God. He was a judge of Israel, and yet, unlike the other judges, he never led an army against the enemy.

Rather, in his own brutish way, he antagonized and brutalized the Philistines (who were Israel's enemies) and thus served God's designs.

The story of Samson dates back to the days of the judges in Israel (before the ascendancy of the kings). Israel was not yet a unified nation, but was rather a loose federation of tribes. They were constantly being attacked by their enemies.

When people would call upon the Lord to deliver them from their distress, he would send them a man or woman to lead them against their enemies. These individuals were the judges.

Samson was chosen by God to be a judge even before his birth. A certain Manoah from the tribe of Dan was married to a woman who was barren. An angel appeared to her announcing that she would become pregnant.

However, he warned her that the child must be a Nazirite, one who was totally dedicated to the Lord. He was never to drink wine or shave his head. The child's name was to be Samson.

Samson grew strong and was full of the Spirit of the Lord. He was so strong that he could kill a lion with his bare hands.

Samson married a Philistine woman. At their wedding feast he challenged the Philistines to a wager concerning a riddle. When his wife betrayed the riddle's solution to them, Samson became enraged. He killed some Philistines and burned their fields.

The Philistines, seeking revenge, killed his wife and her father. They then went after Samson. His fellow Jews handed him over to the Philistines, but he was able to slay them all with the jawbone of an ass.

Samson then married Delilah. She was an evil woman, and she coaxed Samson into telling her the source of his strength. He told her that it was because his hair had never been cut.

When Samson was asleep, Delilah cut off his hair. The Philistines were then able to capture him and torture him, gouging out his eyes and making him do hard labor.

One day the Philistines were holding a feast and they decided to amuse themselves at Samson's expense. They brought him to their temple to make fun of him. When he arrived there, he asked to be placed near the central pillars of the building.

Samson then called upon God to give him back his strength one more time. God did this, and Samson pulled down the pillars, causing the building to collapse on him and all the Philistines. He died as he had lived—violent, but dedicated to the Lord.

# Ruth The Righteous Gentile

*Ruth 1—4*

WE expect a certain loyalty from members of our own family, but when someone who is related to us in a more distant manner goes out of the way to treat us kindly, we are sometimes quite surprised. This type of treatment is, after all, something family members must do, but that is not true of others.

Ruth is one of those people of exceptional character who did much more than what was expected of them. She married an Israelite man who had moved with his family to her homeland, Moab. Her father-in-law had died before the wedding, so Naomi, her mother-in-law was a widow.

Ruth was married about ten years when her husband and his brother both died. Naomi, who was now left childless as well as being bereft of her husband, decided to move back to Bethlehem where some of her family resided. She told her daughters-in-law that they should return to their families (as was the custom in those days).

One of the daughters-in-law did go back to her family, but Ruth refused to do so. She told Naomi, "Where you go, I will go, and where you lodge, I will lodge; your people shall be my people and your God my God."

Ruth traveled with Naomi to Bethlehem. There Naomi sent Ruth into the fields of one of her relatives, Boaz, to glean the grain (pick up the scattered grain after the harvesters). Boaz saw her and inquired about her.

When Boaz found out what a courageous and giving woman Ruth was, he called her over and told her that she should eat and drink along with his hired men. He also ordered the men to respect her.

When Ruth went home, she told Naomi about the kindness of Boaz toward her. Naomi sent her to sleep at Boaz's feet, a sign that she would like him to marry her. Boaz was pleased with that prospect and sent her home with a fine gift to show his willingness to marry her.

Before he could marry Ruth, Boaz had to receive the permission of one of their kinsmen, for that man was a closer relative to Ruth than he. Boaz went to the city gate, and there he received the permission.

Boaz wed Ruth and took her to his home. She soon gave birth to a son whom they named Obed. Her son, Obed, was the grandfather of King David.

The story of Ruth had an obvious lesson for Israelites. They were accustomed to being suspicious of foreigners. Ruth, on the other hand, was a foreigner, a pagan, who was both righteous and a woman of God (and even the ancestress of their greatest king).

The Israelites (and we) are being told that we should not judge people by their nationality, race, color, and the like. Rather we should look at their hearts.

# Hannah     The Mother of Samuel

*1 Samuel 1—2*

THERE are times when, after we have tried everything at our disposition, we know there is really nothing else we can do on our own. It is at those moments that we turn to the One who can accomplish all things; it is then that we place ourselves in the hands of God. Whether God accedes to our request or not, we have grown, for we have trusted in Him.

Hannah experienced this self-abandonment to God's will in her life. She was the wife of a man named Elkanah. Her husband loved her greatly, more than his other wife. Yet, he was helpless when it came to the great misfortune in Hannah's life, for she was barren. This grieved her greatly.

Elkanah frequently professed his great love for her, but this did not really console her. Hannah's misfortune was aggravated even more by the cruel mocking of Elkanah's other wife. In the end she had nowhere to turn.

One year when the family went up to the shrine of God in Shiloh, Hannah placed herself in God's hands. She wept bitterly and prayed to the Lord. She promised Him that if God removed her curse, she would dedicate her son to the service of the Lord.

Eli, the priest at Shiloh, saw her praying, but since he could not hear her words and she appeared to be acting strangely, he accused her of being drunk. She explained herself to him, and rather than thinking ill of her, he blessed her and prayed that God would grant her request.

Shortly after returning home, Hannah conceived and bore a son whom she named Samuel (the name is a sign of her dedicating the child to God, for his name means, "his name is God").

As soon as she had weaned the child, she took him to the shrine in Shiloh and dedicated him to the service of the Lord as she had promised to do.

Once again, Hannah was placing herself totally in God's hands, for Samuel was her only son and she was, in a sense, giving him up. Yet, she felt that she could do nothing else, for all her trust was in God.

God rewarded that trust. He made Samuel, her son, great in all of Israel and gave her five other children.

The second chapter of the first book of Samuel records a psalm attributed to Hannah. This psalm expresses her feelings well, for it tells of how God rescues those who rely upon Him.

The psalm bears much similarity to the *Magnificat,* the hymn of praise sung by Mary to thank God for His wondrous ways. Like the *Magnificat,* it beckons us to trust in God, even when all hope seems futile, for God does not abandon those who trust in Him.

# Samuel     The Judge of Israel

*1 Samuel 1—28*

IT often happens at a major turning point of history that a great man or woman will arise to guide a nation from one experience to another. For Israel during the 11th century B.C., that great figure was Samuel.

Samuel was the last of the judges of Israel. Judges were a mixture of warlord, prophet, and priest. Samuel served in all of these functions. He was chosen from before his birth (as is seen by the miraculous events concerning his birth).

His mother, Hannah, dedicated him to the Lord at the shrine in Shiloh to fulfill the promise she had made. While Samuel was still young the Lord spoke to him for the first time, foretelling the disaster that He would visit upon the family of Eli, the priest.

Samuel led the Israelites into battle, and he also judged their disputes. He was, in effect, the leader of Israel. He was not, however, its king. God alone was King of Israel; Samuel was nothing more than His representative.

There was no real capital, no standing army, no court. The government in those days was nothing more than a loose federation of tribes.

Eventually the Israelites grew tired of that type of arrangement. Without a standing army and the concentration of power around one individual such as a king, they could not effectively defend themselves against their enemies. For that reason they asked Samuel for a king.

At first Samuel opposed this idea for it seemed to him that this was an insult against God, their king. God, however, ordered him to give them what they desired; so Samuel anointed Saul as King of Israel.

For a while Saul did what was pleasing to God, but then he offended the Lord by his actions. He failed to fulfill a promise to totally annihilate the enemy, and he also offered a sacrifice that was to have been offered by Samuel.

Because of these two transgressions, God rejected Saul. He ordered Samuel to go to Bethlehem to anoint a new king. There Samuel visited the family of Jesse and anointed his youngest son, David, as king of Israel.

Saul continued to rule for some time, but he knew that God had rejected him. He became more and more depressed over this fact and possibly even went mad because of it. He always saw Samuel as one who had caused his misfortunes.

Even after Samuel had died Saul continued to fear and yet respect him. Before the battle of Mount Gilboa he had a medium convoke Samuel's spirit so that he could consult with him.

Samuel confirmed Saul's greatest fear: that Saul and his sons would die the next day in battle—the fulfillment of the curse that Samuel had pronounced against Saul and his house.

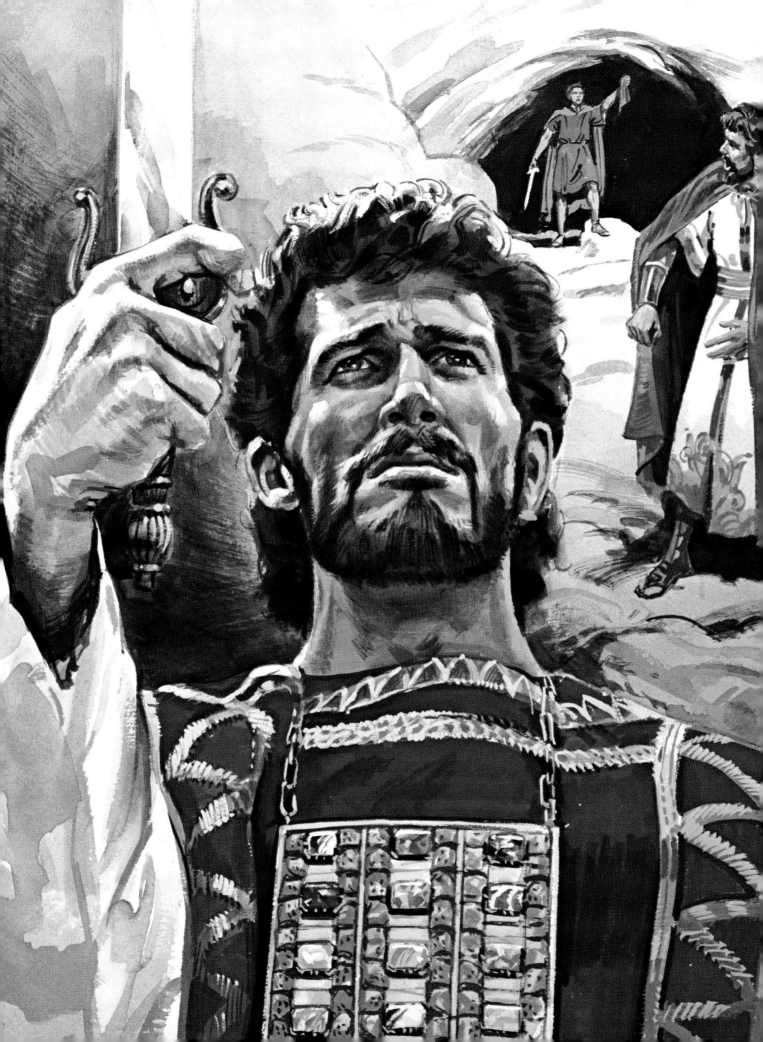

# Saul — The Tragic King

*1 Samuel 8—31*

THERE is something terribly tragic about King Saul. He was chosen by God to be the first king of Israel, but he was just as quickly rejected by God for what seem to have been minor infractions against God's will. His rejection appears to have driven him mad, and he finished his life by striking out in rage against all whom he loved.

Saul was working for his father when the people of Israel decided that they wanted a king. Samuel, the judge, at first rejected their request, but he changed his mind when God commanded him to do as the people had requested.

One day when Saul came to consult with Samuel about some lost animals, Samuel anointed him King of Israel. God's spirit came upon Saul, and he began to prophesy—a sign that he was chosen to be leader by God Himself.

Saul quickly led Israel against their enemies, the Philistines. He and his son Jonathan met with considerable success.

All did not go well, however, for Saul also offended God. He failed to keep his promise to destroy all that the enemy possessed (the ban). Saul also offended God by performing a sacrifice that was to have been performed by Samuel.

Certainly the king had sinned in both cases for he had not been faithful to God and had not trusted in Him. Yet, the punishment almost seems too severe for the sin committed, for God totally rejected him. Saul continued to rule, but God chose David to succeed him. From that moment on Saul's character degenerated, and he became more and more dangerous.

He took David into his service after David killed Goliath. He seems to have genuinely loved David, but he also was jealous of his success. He gave his daughter to him in marriage, but only after he set a price on her which was intended to get David killed.

After the wedding, Saul repeatedly tried to kill his son-in-law. When David fled for his life, the king pursued him and killed those who tried to assist him. Finally David was forced to seek refuge as a mercenary of a Philistine prince.

Once, David cornered a sleeping Saul in a cave and cut off a piece of the king's mantle. Later, he held the piece up for Saul to see, indicating that he could have killed his pursuer but had chosen not to do so.

Saul was killed in battle by the Philistines along with three of his sons. One of his other sons, Ishbaal, tried to rule in Israel while David ruled in Judah, but he was eventually murdered, and David became king of the whole land. Saul and his whole family had been rejected by God, and not one of them was to rule over Israel.

Why was Saul so murderous? Possibly he was mentally unstable, for the Bible speaks of an evil spirit that came over him.

What drove Saul insane? We can't be sure, but it might be that he just could not accept God's will in his life and vehemently resented God's favoritism toward David.

# David — The Chosen King

*1 Samuel 16—31; 2 Samuel 1—24; 1 Kings 1—2*

IN a way, it almost seems as if David was God's fair-haired boy, for it appeared that he could do no wrong. His life, though, was not a totally charmed existence, as will be seen below.

David was only a boy when Samuel, the prophet, anointed him as king (even while Saul was still alive). Sometime after this event, David became a hero by killing Goliath the Philistine, a giant of a man, with a rock from his sling. He ended up at the court of Saul serving first as a court musician and then as a lieutenant in the army.

David enjoyed tremendous success in battle, and his acclaim quickly spread. Saul became jealous of him and on a number of occasions tried to kill him. Two of Saul's children, Jonathan, a good friend to David, and Michal, David's wife, protected him. David fled to the Philistine territory where he lived as a mercenary until Saul died.

When Saul was killed in battle, David was proclaimed king by the southern tribes of Israel, but one of Saul's sons, Ishbaal, was proclaimed king in the north. War ensued and lasted seven years until Ishbaal was assassinated. The tribes then united under David.

David attacked Jerusalem, a pagan city, and conquered it, making it his capital. He moved the ark of the covenant there, thus establishing Jerusalem as the center of cult as well and unifying the nation around this one city.

David went on to defeat his enemies on every side, creating a small empire in the process. He even advanced the culture of his land, as is evidenced by the psalms which are attributed to him.

David's family life, however, was, in many ways, tragic. He fought with his wife Michal and was never reconciled. He committed adultery with Bathsheba and had her husband killed. Their first child died at birth. His eldest son was killed by Absalom (the next oldest) after he raped Absalom's sister. Absalom was killed in a rebellion against David.

Even David's succession was in question for the eldest surviving son, Adonijah, seemed to be taking power before David's death. David squelched his plans by having Solomon, Bathsheba's son, anointed king.

It cannot be said, either, that David was without sin. He committed adultery and murder, wrongfully conducted a census, and even fought with the Philistines against Israel. Yet he always repented for his sins, and God forgave him.

When David asked to build a house for God (a temple), God refused permission (lest David believe that he had done God a favor). Nevertheless, God promised to build a house for David, his dynasty, which would be everlasting. Jesus, the root and sprout of David, is the true fulfillment of that promise, for He is the Eternal King.

# Michal, Abigail, and Bathsheba

*1 Samuel 14—30; 2 Samuel 1—24; 1 Kings 1—2*

ALTHOUGH Michal, Abigail, and Bathsheba were three wives of the same man, King David, they were strikingly different in character and outlook.

Michal, the first of David's wives, was the daughter of King Saul. David, at the time that he married her, was a lieutenant in Saul's army and a hero of many battles. Saul granted him her hand but under the condition that he pay for her with the foreskins of 100 Philistines—a price that Saul hoped would get David killed.

David returned with double the required sum (adding to Saul's jealousy). Michal loved David, and she protected him from the wrath of her father. Eventually, though, David had to flee from Saul, and Saul gave Michal to another man to be his wife.

After Saul was dead, David set the condition of her return to him as a stipulation for peace with the north. She seems to have fallen in love with that second husband, for their parting was sorrowful.

Michal had changed in her attitude toward David for she was now shrewish. She even berated him for his conduct during a festival, and for this David refused to lie with her for the rest of her life.

Abigail was a simple woman. She helped David while he was fleeing from Saul (although her husband had refused to help him). When she was widowed, David took her as his wife.

We don't know much about her, but she is described as being an attractive and sensible woman. One gets the impression that she was a good, uncomplicated woman.

The same thing cannot be said of Bathsheba. She was the wife of Uriah the Hittite, one of David's troops. David saw her bathing, and he lusted for her, committing adultery with her. He also arranged for the death of her husband so that he could marry her.

Nathan, the prophet, condemned David for this and pronounced the judgment that the child would die. Shortly after the death of that first child, though, Bathsheba became pregnant again and bore another child, Solomon.

When David was dying, Bathsheba conspired with Nathan and other court officials to convince him to name Solomon as his successor, even though Solomon wasn't David's eldest. David named her son as coregent and thus assured his position as David's successor.

Bathsheba was not the courtly and refined lover that Michal was, nor was she a simple, good woman like Abigail. She gives the impression of being a seductive, passionate lover, cunning when her own interests or those of her son were at stake.

Yet Bathseba wasn't really a wicked woman like Jezebel. She was an earthly woman, one in whom humanity and its weakness were very apparent.

# Nathan   The Court Prophet

*2 Samuel 7:1-17; 12:1-25; 1 Kings 1—2*

WE often think of prophets as being individuals who foretold the future. Although it is true that they occasionally did that, they had a much more important function in Israel.

It was their duty to help the Israelites understand how God saw and judged reality. They were, in a sense, a cross between being a court counselor and the conscience of the nation.

Nathan fits that role of prophet very well. He was the court prophet under David.

Nothing is known of Nathan's background, and he only appears three times in the account of David's reign, but it is difficult to miss his importance.

The first mention of Nathan has to do with David's plan to build a temple.

David had decided that since he had built a palace for himself, it was only fitting that he should build a house for the Lord (a temple). He consulted Nathan to see if God was pleased with his plan.

At first Nathan encouraged David, but then he had a vision in which God disapproved of the plan. In that vision God told David that it was not David who would build a house for him but He who would build a house for David (a dynasty).

God probably did not want David to build the temple because David was beginning to develop an attitude of superiority toward God, as if he could do God a favor by building Him a house. God reminded David of who was in charge.

Nathan appears again to condemn David for his adulterous rapport with Bathsheba and his murder of her husband, Uriah the Hittite.

Nathan got his point across by telling a beautiful parable to David which made David indignant at the villain of the story.

Nathan then told David that he was, in fact, the culprit. He pronounced God's punishment upon David—that the child who had been conceived in adultery would die.

Nathan then reappears when David is old and dying.

On this occasion, the prophet sided with Bathsheba, Zadok the priest, and Beniah the soldier to further the cause of Bathsheba's son, Solomon.

Nathan persuaded Bathsheba to intercede for her son with David so that he would make Solomon his heir. Their plan was successful and Solomon was anointed as coregent while David was still alive.

This role of prophet and counselor did not die with the Old Testament. We still need people in our lives who remind us of what God wants us to do. We need people to whom we can go to ask counsel. If we try to live without them, we can easily lose our way.

It does not matter if such persons are spiritual directors or confessors or just good friends, as long as we are sure that they will help us to see what is good and pleasing to God.

# Solomon     The Wise Man of God

*2 Samuel 12:25; 1 Kings 1—11*

HOW does one gauge the success of rulers? Is it a question of how great they make their nations or how prosperous? Does it depend upon their astuteness in politics? Is it a question of their moral responsibility? Their cultural sense? All of these questions could be asked of rulers, and they provide some indications of the successes and failures.

Was Solomon a great ruler according to these criteria? He was in certain ways, but in others he was a failure. Solomon is best known for being a wise man. When given the opportunity by God of asking for anything, he asked for wisdom.

Solomon used that wisdom in governing the people justly (as seen in his famous judgment of the two women who claimed to be mother of the same child). He advanced the cultural level of his country, for his reign was a golden age for Hebrew literature.

During Solomon's reign the country was at peace. Solomon kept the country strong by enlarging the military.

The kingdom underwent an explosion of construction during his reign. The climax of that movement was the construction of the temple. He also oversaw the construction of several garrison cities for his army as well as a fleet for trading and a copper mine. The country had never been so prosperous.

However, all was not perfect in the kingdom. The explosion of building in Israel had to be financed in some way, and it seems as if Solomon used two techniques: taxes and forced labor.

The Israelites bitterly resented these two impositions for they bled the economy dry.

Furthermore, the prosperity in the nation was illusory. While some were very wealthy, the masses were living in great poverty.

These resentments would explode after Solomon's death with the result that only two of the twelve tribes agreed to follow his successor. The other ten tribes chose their own king and became an independent nation.

On a religious level, also, Solomon would receive mixed grades. He helped to spawn a great flourishing of religious literature, and he built the magnificent temple.

On the other hand, he married foreign princesses and not only let them worship their foreign gods but even promoted the cult of these gods.

Solomon built shrines to those pagan gods on a hill opposite Jerusalem which even to this day is called the hill of shame because of what Solomon did there.

Was he a great king? It is difficult to answer. Like all of us, he used some of his God-given talent well (e.g., his wisdom, his culture), but all too often he fell short of the greatness that could have been his had he been more faithful to God's call.

# Elijah     "My God is Yahweh"

*1 Kings 17—19; 21; 2 Kings 1:1—2:18*

WE often assume that Israel was faithful to Yahweh and that only occasionally did it slip into idolatry. Actually, the opposite is closer to the truth. During most of Israel's history there was a running battle between Yahweh and the Canaanite god, Baal, to see whom Israel would serve.

This battle became critical during the reign of King Ahab of Israel (c. 869-850 B.C.). Ahab's wife, Jezebel, was a princess from Sidon, a pagan city, and she wanted her gods to be the gods of Israel.

It was in this context that Elijah prophesied. Elijah predicted a three-year drought (proving that Yahweh produced rain and not Baal).

The Lord protected Elijah first by having a raven bring him food and then by sending him to a widow (whose food supply the Lord miraculously replenished). Elijah, repaying the widow for her kindness, raised her son from the dead.

At the end of the drought Elijah challenged the priests of Baal to a contest. They would both call upon their gods to send fire to consume their sacrifices. The god who answered would be the god of Israel.

The prophets of Baal called in vain, but when Elijah called upon Yahweh, fire immediately descended from the heavens. Elijah then ordered that the priests of Baal be killed.

Jezebel was furious and sought revenge. Elijah fled to Mount Horeb where he called upon the Lord. The Lord answered him, ordering him to choose a successor for the kings of Damascus and Israel and to name Elisha as his own successor.

In this appearance, Elijah saw an earthquake, wind, and then lightning, but the Lord was not in them. He then heard a gentle breeze, and the Lord was in the breeze (showing that the Lord often works in gentle ways).

Elijah's next prophetic action was to condemn the house of Ahab for Jezebel's murderous seizure of the vineyard of Naboth. He also condemned Ahab's successor, Ahaziah, for appealing to a pagan god during his illness. Ahaziah sent troops to arrest Elijah, but the Lord again protected him by consuming the troops with fire.

Elijah's career ended with his passing on his prophetic authority to his successor, Elisha, and his being carried off into the heavens in a fiery chariot. Throughout his life he had been a selfless defender of the cult of his Lord, Yahweh.

It was believed that Elijah would return before the coming of the Messiah. This is why John the Baptist is called another Elijah, and why Elijah appears along with Moses during Jesus' Transfiguration on Mount Tabor.

# Jezebel     The Evil Woman

*1 Kings 16:31; 18; 19; 21:5—15; 2 Kings 9:29-37*

HER name is synonymous with wanton, for Jezebel is the woman who through seduction and enticements tried to deceive all with whom she came in contact. She was not satisfied with drawing her husband, the King of Israel, into sin, but she even tried with all of her might to wrest the whole nation away from the Lord.

For this she became infamous, and she suffered the full consequences of her sin.

Jezebel was the daughter of the king of Sidon. Her father was a priest of the pagan god, Baal.

Ahab, the King of Israel, married her in a political marriage. He desperately needed an alliance with Sidon to protect Israel from the power of Syria. In marrying her, though, he showed that he placed more trust in politics than in the help of the Lord.

This alliance had disastrous consequences. Jezebel sought to promote the cult of Baal, even supporting a school of prophets of Baal. At the same time, she sought to suppress the cult of Yahweh. The first book of Kings recounts how she arranged for the death of all the prophets of the Lord except Elijah. He proved to be her nemesis.

Elijah prophesied a three-year drought that the Lord would bring upon Israel to punish it for its rebellion. He then challenged the priests of Baal to a test. They lost the test showing that they were false prophets, and they were put to death.

Jezebel was furious and vowed revenge, but she did not succeed in her plans. It was, in fact, she who would die in a brutal manner. Her death was prophesied by Elijah as a punishment for her crime against Naboth.

Naboth owned a vineyard that Ahab, Jezebel's husband, wanted. Naboth refused to cede it to him, so Jezebel arranged for his death. She had false witnesses testify against Naboth and put him to death. Ahab was then able to confiscate the land.

When Elijah found out about this he confronted them with their crime and pronounced sentence against Ahab, Jezebel, and their entire family.

The prophecy was fulfilled during the rebellion of Jehu. He came to the palace, and there Jezebel was waiting for him dressed in a scandalous manner so that she might seduce him. Even at this point she was relying on deception and lust.

Jehu ordered her put to death, and the judgment was carried out by the palace aids (who threw her out the window). Her body laid in the courtyard where it was eaten by the dogs of the city (even as Elijah had prophesied).

The punishment that Jezebel suffered was not so much one God inflicted upon her as one she brought upon herself. She had brought death to Israel through her deceptions and sorcery, and for that she was doomed to die.

# Elisha    The Wonder-Worker

*1 Kings 19—22; 2 Kings 1—13.*

WHEN we write or speak about those we love and respect, we usually tend to emphasize their positive aspects and ignore their shortcomings. If such people are especially talented, we might even be tempted to make it seem as if they are superhuman.

We get the impression that this has happened in the case of Elisha the prophet. His story seems to be a series of his wonders and miracles. We never really get to know Elisha as a person.

The reason for this is that the story of Elisha was not produced by an impartial source. It was written by some of his disciples who deeply respected him.

Elisha's disciples wanted to show everyone how great their master was. The result is that they only give us a caricature of the man's greatness.

Elisha's penchant for greatness was inherited from his own master, Elijah. Elijah called him to be a prophet near the end of his own career, and he invested him with a double portion of his spirit before he was taken up into the heavens.

Elisha continued many of the same activities that his master had performed. He was involved in the politics of his own land and of the neighboring states of Judah and Syria. He fought injustice and immorality when he saw them (e.g., punishing his disciple for cheating Naaman the Syrian). He reached out to people beyond his own borders and rewarded their goodness to him (e.g., when he raised the son of the Shunammite woman).

Even more than Elijah, he seemed very concerned for the welfare of those close to him. He was constantly performing miracles to help them in their difficulties.

One of the best known of the stories about Elisha involves Naaman the Syrian. Naaman was an important general in the army of the King of Syria, but he was also a leper. One of his servants, a young Jewish captive, recommended to him that he go to Elisha to seek a cure.

Naaman went to the prophet, showing him great honor, but Elisha refused to exit from his house. Rather, he sent word to Naaman that he should bathe in the Jordan River seven times.

Naaman was infuriated by Elisha's disrespect toward him and his failure to miraculously heal him. He almost refused to go to the Jordan but was then convinced by his servants that he should give it a try.

Upon washing in the Jordan Naaman was healed of his leprosy. This taught him that God often works in very ordinary ways.

This is something that we should keep in mind when we are looking for God's presence in our own lives. Like Elisha's disciples, we should be ready to see God present and active in those around us and even in ourselves.

# Amos    Herald of Social Justice

*Amos 1—9*

WHEN we think of the prophets, we often picture them as being educated and powerful men. That, however, doesn't hold true for Amos, for he was neither rich nor powerful.

He was a poor shepherd from the southern kingdom of Judah who did not even exercise his mission in his own country, but rather was sent by the Lord to preach in the northern kingdom of Israel.

Nonetheless, Amos's anger at the social injustice that he witnessed blazed eloquently, and his message reached even the most powerful in Israel.

It was so important, in fact, that Amos became the first of the prophets to have his oracles collected together in a single book.

All of this is true despite the fact that his prophetic career probably lasted no more than a few months.

Amos began his prophecy like many of the other prophets of his day, by condemning Israel's enemies and predicting their demise on the "Day of the Lord," the day of the Lord's judgment.

However, the prophet surprised his audience by not stopping with Israel's enemies. Instead, he went on and condemned Israel and Judah, for their injustice was just as bad.

In a sense, they were even more guilty than the pagans, for they had been chosen by the Lord. Yet, they dared to presume God's favor.

Israel's greatest sin was social injustice. This was a time of great prosperity, but only the rich were able to enjoy it. The poor were more desperate than ever. Those who should have warned the rich about their sinfulness—the princes, prophets, and priests said nothing, and by their silence they became their collaborators.

They even turned the liturgy into a mockery. Even while they were offering many and great sacrifices, they were plotting their next injustice. By doing this they were implicitly stating that God approved of all that they were doing.

For all of this Amos bitterly condemned Israel. He warned them that the Day of the Lord would be the day of their own judgment, and they would suffer terribly. There would be no escape. God would no longer accept their half-hearted conversions.

Amos's message was rejected (chapter 7), but his words would not die. When Israel fell to her enemies, his prophecy provided the explanation as to why God would allow the disaster to occur—it was a punishment for sin.

A later author added several verses to Amos's prophecy which completed his message (9:11ff), for after the punishment God would restore His people. God's anger was not really destructive, but rather it was a cleansing anger that would bring His people back to Him.

# Hosea    Parable of the Love of God

*Hosea 1—14*

TO be in love is a great thing, but it is also something that leaves us terribly vulnerable. We place ourselves in the power of another who has the capacity to betray us if he or she so wishes.

Hosea, the prophet, realized fully the risk involved in love. His wife, Gomer, was a prostitute. He deeply loved her and wished nothing else of her than that she be faithful to him.

Every time that Gomer would go off to her lovers, Hosea would be deeply hurt. Yet every time that she went away, he would call her back to himself and forgive her.

In a way, Hosea made a fool of himself over Gomer. It was obvious to all that she could never be faithful to him, yet he constantly gave her the chance to reform her life. His love was too great to allow him to give up on her.

As Hosea reflected upon his misfortunes, he came to the realization that his plight was not unlike that of God. God deeply loved Israel and wanted nothing of her other than her love and fidelity, but she proved over and over again that she was incapable of fidelity.

Israel was continuously turning away from following God and choosing to follow the false gods of the Canaanites. No matter how many times God would call her, forgive her, chastise her, she would nevertheless forget Him and chase once more after her lovers (the false gods).

Seeing the similarities between his plight and that of God, Hosea wrote about his life so that his story would be a parable for Israel. He, like Amos who wrote shortly before Hosea, warned Israel that she would have to pay a price for her infidelity. She was risking the possibility that God would divorce her completely.

Hosea also used another familial image in composing his prophecy. He spoke of Israel as a foolish son who was being born.

The pains of childbirth had arrived (the chastisements that God had sent to warn Israel about its errant ways), but the foolish son had ignored the pains and refused to be born (the Israelites refused to change their ways). For that reason, he was doomed to die.

These dire warnings were not to be heeded. Israel continued in its obstinate ways, and God visited His wrath upon it.

God allowed the Assyrians to invade and destroy it. Yet God did not totally abandon Israel.

Even as Hosea recognized, God would never abandon His beloved forever. He would preserve a remnant of those who would remain faithful to Him, and these He would raise up. God loved Israel too much to allow its infidelity to defeat His love.

# Isaiah   Prophet of the Holy God

*Isaiah 1—39; 2 Kings 19:20—20:19*

THE manner in which a prophet is called by God often determines the type of message he preaches. Isaiah is an example of this. His vocation is reported in Isaiah 6:1ff, a vision in which he experienced the great holiness of God and his own insignificance and sinfulness.

God purified him of that sinfulness (as with a burning coal), and for the rest of his life Isaiah was a herald of God's holiness. Holiness was the core of his message whether he spoke of questions of morality, worship, or politics.

Isaiah addressed his message to the kings of Judah. The first chapters of his book report his dealings with King Ahaz. He counseled Ahaz not to fear when Judah was invaded by Israel and Syria, but to trust in the Lord alone. Ahaz refused and sought aid from Assyria.

Isaiah offered Ahaz a sign from the Lord, but the king refused it, so Isaiah responded with the prophecy, "The maiden [virgin] shall conceive and bear a son, and shall call his name Immanuel" (7:14). Isaiah was referring to a child in his own generation, but the Holy Spirit had a more profound meaning in mind: the virgin birth of Jesus.

Ahaz silenced Isaiah, and he refrained from prophesying for the next fifteen years. When Hezekiah ascended to the throne, Isaiah began to prophesy again.

Hezekiah was a good king, and Isaiah predicted that he marked a new beginning, one which would see the birth of a new king who would bring peace to Israel and all of creation (chapters 9 and 11).

When Hezekiah contemplated rebelling against Assyria and seeking the assistance of Egypt, Isaiah warned him not to trust in humans but to trust in the Holy One, God. He imitated the exiles from a neighboring city that had trusted in Egypt and had been defeated (chapter 20).

The rest of Isaiah's prophetic ministry was concerned with this problem and the importance of trusting in God.

It is possible that Isaiah was martyred under Hezekiah's successor, Manasseh, the most evil king in the history of Judah.

Large portions of the book bearing Isaiah's name were not actually written by him. He wrote most of the first 39 chapters, but chapters 40—65 are the product of two later authors.

Chapters 40—55 were written by an anonymous author during the exile commonly called Deutero-Isaiah (Second Isaiah). The theme of that section is consolation and a promise of new hope to the nations suffering in Babylon.

Chapters 56—65 were written by an author called Trito-Isaiah (or Third Isaiah) sometime after the exile. His theme was that while Israel was guilty of sin, yet God would give Israel a new beginning, a new creation, a prophecy fulfilled in the new covenant of Jesus.

# Micah    The Prophet of Bethlehem

*Micah 1—7*

I T is difficult to speak about Micah the prophet because so little is known about him. We do know that he prophesied around 700 B.C. and that he was born in southwest Judea, but little else is certain. Even the book that bears his name is not entirely his production, for large sections of it seem to be later additions. His message is not especially original, being quite similar to that of Amos, Hosea, and Isaiah.

Yet, in spite of all this, his message was preserved and is considered to be important for several verses speak of Bethlehem, the birthplace of the Messiah.

Like Hosea, Micah condemned idolatry. Like Amos, he declaimed the social injustice of his day. The rich had built up large plantations while the poor were left landless. They bought justice from those who should have defended the weak.

The prophet proclaimed that for these sins Israel must be punished. Yet, the punishment would not be without hope. Micah prophesied that a remnant would remain who would continue to be faithful to the Lord, and this remnant would be blessed.

Micah's most famous verses are contained in chapter 5: "You, Bethlehem-Ephrathah, too small to be among the clans of Judah, from you shall come forth for me one who is to be ruler in Israel; whose origin is from of old, from ancient times." Interestingly, Micah probably did not intend the meaning which was later attached to these words.

Micah intended to contrast two cities: Jerusalem and Bethlehem. Jerusalem was the center of the nation—a powerful city. It could rely on the fact that it had been chosen by God as His dwelling place on earth (the city of the Temple).

Bethlehem, on the other hand, was a small, weak town. It had no power of its own on which it could rely, so it had to depend entirely on the Lord. It was also the city of David. David was the weakest of Jesse's sons, and yet the Lord chose him to be King.

By saying these words, Micah was stating that those who depended on their own power, like Jerusalem, were doomed, but those who trusted in the power of the Lord would be raised up.

The Holy Spirit added a meaning to these words that even Micah didn't realize they contained. Sometime before the birth of Jesus, this prophecy came to be understood as pointing to Bethlehem as the birthplace of the coming Messiah.

Thus, when Jesus was born, He was seen to be that King about whom Micah spoke. Jesus, in fact, encompassed both meanings, for He was both the Messiah and the sign that God came to those who are weak and who trust in Him.

# Jeremiah — Prophet of New Covenant

*Jeremiah 1—52*

FEW people ever realize the full significance of the invitation to take up one's cross and follow the Lord. Jeremiah, the prophet, seems to be one of those few, for his prophetic vocation involved tremendous sacrifice for the sake of the kingdom.

Jeremiah prophesied during the reigns of King Josiah and his successors. These were troubled times for Judah—critical times that ended with the defeat of Judah by the Babylonian forces and the great exile. Jeremiah's mission during this crisis was to preach repentance.

The prophet condemned the iniquity of the people and their readiness to turn away from God. He warned them that unless they returned to the Lord, they would suffer the consequences of their acts. Like Isaiah who had prophesied during a previous crisis, Jeremiah beseeched them to trust in the Lord alone.

Jeremiah deeply loved his people and their land. He desired with all his heart that they would repent, but they did not. Rather, they scorned the word of the Lord addressed to them through Jeremiah. They accused him of disloyalty toward the nation.

Under King Jehoiakim Jeremiah was thrown in prison and accused of blasphemy for foretelling the coming destruction of Jerusalem. When released, he seems to have been forbidden to prophesy in the temple. He sent Baruch, his secretary, to continue his ministry there, but even that was short-lived. The king confiscated the scroll with Jeremiah's prophecies and burned it.

During the reign of Zedekiah, Jehoiakim's successor, the chief princes of Jerusalem conspired to kill Jeremiah, throwing him in an empty cistern to starve to death. Even after the fall of Jerusalem Jeremiah suffered.

When the Babylonian governor of Judah was assassinated, Jeremiah advised the people not to flee to Egypt. They ignored his advice and forced him and Baruch to accompany them (and he died there.)

Jeremiah agonized over the fact that he, a man totally devoted to God, should have to suffer so much. He suffered both in having to prophesy against his beloved land and in being persecuted by his enemies. Eventually, though, he realized that no matter what happened, the Lord was with him.

He was further consoled by the message of hope that the Lord had him address to the nation. He believed that there would be days of destruction, but he prayed that this disaster would bring His people around and they would convert.

In that day the Lord would establish a new covenant with them, one not written on stone like the covenant of Moses, but written on their very hearts. They would each know and love God and be totally His, never to stray again.

# Ezekiel    Prophet of New Life

*Ezekiel 1—48*

A PRIEST who lived in exile in Babylon, Ezekiel served as a hinge between two eras of Israelite history. He had been carried off to Babylon during the first exile of 597 B.C., and he was already there when the temple was destroyed and great numbers of citizens were deported.

Ezekiel's prophecies, like those of Jeremiah, left no doubt that the disaster that befell Judah was caused by sinfulness. He reviewed the entire history of the Jewish people and concluded that it was nothing but a history of incessant rebellion and that the holiness of God demanded punishment.

The prophet rejected the view that the innocent were being punished for the sins of the nation. He argued instead that each person was responsible for his or her own sinfulness and its consequent punishment.

Ezekiel stressed the point that he, as a prophet, had the sacred responsibility of calling the people to conversion. If he reneged in this task, he would be held accountable for the sins of those to whom he failed to preach. In all of this, Ezekiel resembled Jeremiah.

However, Ezekiel differed from Jeremiah in his emphasis on the future. It is possible that he did this because he was prophesying from a different perspective. Jeremiah prophesied shortly before the exile and at its very beginning, and his message is generally pessimistic.

Ezekiel's prophetic career extended further into the exile. The people had already realized their sinfulness, and now they needed a message of consolation.

Ezekiel promised that God would renew His people. He promised them a new heart and a new spirit. No longer would they follow the Lord under compulsion. Now they would lovingly obey the law of the Lord.

This restoration is symbolized by the vision of the dry bones. The Lord led Ezekiel out to a valley covered with dry bones. He then had him prophesy that the Spirit of God would enter the bones. When Ezekiel did this, they were clothed in flesh and came to life.

Israel would be like these bones. Now she was dead in sin, but soon she would be filled with the Spirit of God and be alive again.

The last chapters of Ezekiel's book speak of the coming restoration. All of Israel's enemies would be defeated. The city and the temple that had been destroyed would be wondrously rebuilt. The presence of the Lord would once again be found in the Holy of Holies.

The land would be redistributed to all the tribes, and the entire land would be nourished by a stream of life-giving water that would spring from the temple. All of this is symbolic of the new and abundant life that the Lord was offering His beloved people.

# Deutero-Isaiah and Trito-Isaiah

*Isaiah 40—65*

IT IS odd that although two sacred writers of the Old Testament wrote some of the most beautiful and important verses in the Old Testament, we do not even possess their proper names. We are not exactly sure of when or where they produced their prophecies. Yet in spite of all this, their words have endured and prospered.

Known as Deutero- and Trito-Isaiah, or Second and Third Isaiah, these two men wrote many decades after the original Isaiah. That First Isaiah was the inspiration for much of what they wrote, but because of changed conditions and different literary styles being adopted, the expression of their message varies considerably from that of the First Isaiah.

That is, in fact, how scholars determined that the book of Isaiah has three authors. Its three sections were so different in style and message that it was as if three short stories had been joined together in one book. Even if there were no actual separations between the three stories, anyone reading the book would know what had been done.

The original Isaiah probably wrote from 742 to 701 B.C. The tone of most of the book is one of anger.

Isaiah condemned the nations that were harassing Judah, but he also condemned Judah for its reliance on earthly powers rather than trusting in the Lord. His prophecies go from chapter 1 to 39 in the present book of Isaiah.

Beginning with chapter 40, we find the words of Deutero-Isaiah. This author probably wrote his prophecies during the exile and his message is simple: be consoled.

He told the people who were suffering in exile that God would soon visit them and set them free. They would have a great restoration, a second exodus. They would once again serve the Holy God in their promised land.

Deutero-Isaiah also included in his prophecies the poems about the suffering servant of Yahweh—a servant whose suffering brings forgiveness for the sins of the people. These poems were applied to Jesus by the authors of the Gospels.

Trito-Isaiah, the third of the authors of the book of Isaiah (chapters 56—65), wrote his work at least a century after Deutero-Isaiah. Although he had already seen the Jews return from exile, he also saw that God meant more for His people than a simple liberation from a foreign power.

There would be new heavens and a new earth. All that was old and corrupt would pass away. All humanity would be able to serve the Lord in glory.

The New Testament authors recognized that the new creation proposed by Trito-Isaiah was fulfilled in Jesus who by His death and resurrection made all things new.

# Ezra    The Reformer

*Ezra 1—10; Nehemiah 1—13*

IF we were to be given a choice between living a life of comfort under the domination of a foreign power and living a life of dire poverty but in liberty, it might be difficult for us to choose which we would prefer.

This is the choice that the Jews had to face at the end of the exile. For several decades they had lived in exile in Babylon. Their exile, though, was not a total disaster. They were allowed a certain amount of freedom in their new land to buy and sell, to educate their young, and so on. Many of the Jews even prospered in Babylon.

When Cyrus of Persia defeated Babylon and decided to allow the Jews to return to their homeland, many were not so sure that they wanted to go back. Most, in fact, had not even been born there.

Furthermore, reports of the abysmal living conditions in Palestine had reached Babylon. They would be giving up so much to march off into the unknown.

Therefore it is no surprise that when the caravans withdrew for Palestine, the majority of the Jews in Babylon did not join them.

To devout Jews, this was a scandal. One of these, the priest Ezra, dedicated himself to bringing Jews back to their rightful homeland and restoring Jewish cultural life there.

Even when the Jews reached Palestine, they tended to compromise their values. They were not very careful in keeping the law, and they began to intermarry with foreigners. Ezra saw that this could not continue.

If Jews did not observe the law and they intermarried, then they would become like any other nation on the earth. The Jews, who were a chosen people, were in danger of becoming common.

Ezra, upon arriving in Jerusalem, called the people together and ordered that the law be proclaimed in their midst. This public reading was a type of promulgation of the law so that all who heard it and affirmed it would be bound to live according to its precepts.

This commitment had immediate consequences for Ezra ordered that all who had married foreign women should send them away with their children.

Ezra called upon the Jews of his age to make hard choices. He saw that too many compromises could lead to a weakening of commitment to the point that people are no longer what they say they are.

His example is a powerful reminder to us today that we must, at times, reject the messages that our permissive society gives. We cannot live selfishly, thinking only of our pleasure or success or money.

We must rather try to live a life of love and self-sacrifice. We must be willing to pay the price of fidelity, no matter how high it might be.

# Joel — The Apocalyptic Prophet

*Joel 1—4*

IT IS not always easy to understand what the prophets are trying to tell us in their prophecies. They wrote long ago and in styles of writing that are no longer used.

Those who adopted the style of writing called apocalyptic are especially difficult to decipher. The images that they used are strange, and most of the action described in their books is symbolic. One is never quite sure what is to be taken literally and what is merely figurative.

The book of Revelation is one example of this style.

Joel is one of the prophets of the Old Testament who used the apocalyptic style of writing. Because of this, it is very difficult to figure out what he meant to say.

Chapters 1 and 2 of his book, for example, speak of an invasion of locusts that would devastate the land. It is not clear if he wants us to understand this as actual locusts or something else.

Joel could, for example, be talking about some terrible invasion by a foreign army whose troops seemed to be as numerous as locusts and whose destruction left the land as if it had been eaten bare by locusts.

Even if this is an army, we could still interpret the passage in two different ways. It might be an actual historical army that marched or would march through Palestine or it might be an army of the forces of the Lord that would come in the end times (or the Day of the Lord).

Given this uncertainty about this meaning, what can we say for certain about the prophecy of Joel? It is clear that Joel believed that God had sent or was sending a disaster to force His people to repent.

Joel called upon the people of the Lord to "rend your hearts and not your garments." When they would turn back to God, He would forgive them and remove the chastisement that He had brought upon them.

The enemies of God's people, however, would not escape so easily. They had preyed upon God's chosen ones when He was angry with them, and they had become arrogant in their evil practices. For this God would grievously afflict them.

In speaking of the day of judgment Joel used the following words: "And it shall come to pass afterward, that I will pour out my spirit on all flesh; your sons and your daughters shall prophesy, your old men shall dream dreams and your young men shall see visions."

These are the same words that Peter spoke on the day of Pentecost for Jesus was the judgment come into the world calling all to decide for all times to live for or against God.

# Jonah    In the Belly of the Whale

*2 Kings 14:25; Jonah 1—4; Matthew 12:39-41; Luke 11:29-32*

WHEN we speak of Jonah, one thing must be understood immediately: the story of Jonah is not historical. There are so many contradictions between what is reported in this book and what we know to be true archaeological evidence that it is certain that the story is fictional.

This does not mean, however, that it is worthless, for it presents an important message. It is a parable loosely based on an historical figure (the Jonah mentioned in the Second Book of Kings). Its message is that God wills the salvation of all, and not just of the Jews.

The story begins with Jonah being called by Yahweh to preach conversion to the city of Nineveh (the Assyrian capital). Jonah chafed at that commission for he considered the Ninevites to be evil, and he would have preferred to see them die.

To avoid the deplorable task of converting them, Jonah fled on a ship. When the ship was threatened by a great storm, the sailors cast lots to see whose fault this disaster was. The lot pointed to Jonah, and they threw him overboard.

Jonah was saved from drowning by God who had a great fish swallow him. He remained in the belly of the fish for three days and then was vomited up onto shore. Realizing that he could no longer avoid his duty, he went into Nineveh to preach the coming destruction.

That which Jonah feared most soon occurred, for the King called a great fast and all the people converted their ways. On account of this, the Lord saved them from the predicted destruction.

Jonah was enraged that this people should be saved, and he went off to the east of the city where he built a hut for himself. A gourd plant grew over him and provided him with shade. He found the plant pleasant, and when a worm attacked it and killed it, he was once again furious.

God then spoke to him asking him how he could care so much about a plant that he did not even plant when he showed so little compassion for the people of Nineveh whose greatest fault was that they lived in ignorance.

This book is a lesson to the Jews who had begun to consider themselves superior to the pagans, as well as to us today when we start to become self-righteous. It is a reminder that God loves all people and gave up His Son to die for all of them. We should desire their salvation and not their destruction.

Jonah's name is found in the Gospels when Jesus was asked what sign He would give to demonstrate His authority. Jesus responded that He would give no sign other than that of Jonah.

By this Jesus meant that just as Jonah was in the belly of the fish for three days and was rescued from death, so also the Son of Man would be in the belly of the earth for three days, but the Father would rescue Him from death in the resurrection.

# Job  The Man Who Challenged God

*Job 1—42*

WE have all heard the saying, "the patience of Job." This saying is ironic, for if we read the book of Job carefully, we see that this is one of the few virtues Job did not, in fact, possess. If anything, we are astonished at his impertinence and almost blasphemous indictment of God.

Job is described as being a just man in the opening chapters of the book bearing his name. God was well pleased with him and rewarded him with happiness and riches.

Satan provoked God by saying that the only reason Job was religious was because God had treated him so well. If, on the other hand, Job were to suffer misfortune, he would abandon God.

God then permitted Satan to test Job, and Satan arranged for disaster after disaster to befall Job, until he sat alone on a dung heap, inconsolable in his pain.

Three of Job's friends heard about his misfortunes and came to try to console him. At first they sat in silence, but when Job complained about his fate, they decided to help their friend see the error of his judgment.

They were convinced that God would never cause the suffering of an innocent man, so they assumed that he was guilty of some hidden fault. Thus, totally ignoring the horrendous agony of their friend, they decided to instruct him on their theories about the rapport of God and human beings.

Even this would not have been so bad but the bottom line of their theories was that all this pain was Job's own fault—a conclusion with which Job could not agree. Job knew in his heart of hearts that he was an innocent man.

The debate raged on until Job had finally refuted all of his friends' arguments. In the course of his pronouncements, Job acknowledged that he might have committed some fault that even he did not know about, but he did not see that as a valid reason for his pain.

Job challenged God to appear and debate with him face to face—otherwise he would assume that God was no better than a tyrant.

God finally did appear to answer Job. His answer was odd, for He didn't respond directly but rather manifested His majesty. After showing Job all His power and wonder, He asked Job if He could do the same things that He does.

Job was overawed and acknowledged that God was too great for him. He concluded that one must trust in God no matter what, for God is all-knowing and all-powerful. He could do nothing else than place himself in God's hands.

Job gives us a powerful example of being honest with God and yet, when push comes to shove, trusting in His love.

# Judas Maccabee

**The Hammer of God**

*1 Maccabees 2:1—9:22; 2 Maccabees 1—15*

ALEXANDER the Great is famous for conquering most of the known world by his thirtieth birthday, but most people know little about what happened to his empire after his death.

It was divided among three of his generals with Palestine (the home of the Jews) being ceded to the Ptolemies of Egypt. Soon afterward, though, Palestine passed to the Seleucid empire of Syria.

One of the Seleucid emperors, Antiochus Epiphanes, resolved to force all of his subjects to adopt Greek customs, including the Greek gods. The Jews obstinately opposed this program, but Antiochus applied greater and greater pressure (e.g., the death penalty for circumcising children).

A certain priest, Mattathias, fled Jerusalem with his sons because of these policies. Even in their home city of Modein, though, they came face to face with the persecution, and they refused to compromise.

They killed an official of the emperor and a Jewish collaborator and fled into the mountains, inviting like-minded Jews to follow them. There they gathered strength and expertise.

When Mattathias died in 166 B.C., he left his son Judas Maccabbe (his surname means hammer) in charge of the rebellion. Over the next few years, Judas led his forces into several battles against superior forces and emerged victorious. His first two opponents, Appolonius and Seron, commanded local pagan forces, and they were soundly defeated. Antiochus then sent his own forces under Gorgias and Lysias.

Before going into battle with them, Judas roused his troops by telling them, "It is better for us to die in battle than to witness the ruin of our nation and our sanctuary." God led Judas to victory over this army as well.

This victory gave Judas the possibility to purify the temple that Antiochus had desecrated. He rebuilt the altar and ordered a feast to occur for the temple rededication (Hanukkah).

Judas then made war against several local menaces, rescuing Jews who were imperiled by the Gentiles. Lysias once again attacked, this time defeating Judas. A rebellion in the palace prevented him from finishing Judas off.

Nicanor, another general, attacked too, but Judas defeated him. Finally, Bacchides attacked with a much larger force and defeated Judas, killing him in battle.

Even though Bacchides defeated Judas in battle, he could not kill his spirit. The enthusiasm and courage that Judas had shown inspired his people so that they continued their rebellion until they were finally granted independence.

Before and after his battles Judas would place himself in God's hands, for he recognized that it was the Lord who delivered his enemies into his hands. Judas truly was the hammer of God.

# Daniel  The Man in the Lions' Den

*Daniel 1—14*

DURING times of persecution, it can be difficult to keep up our courage and remain faithful to our beliefs. Often, though, a few words of encouragement can be enough to embolden us and allow us to do that which is heroic.

This was the purpose of the author of the book of Daniel—to offer consolation and encouragement. This book is a series of stories that recount the exploits of a certain Daniel who lived during the Babylonian exile. However, the book was written much later than that, probably during the persecution of Antiochus Epiphanes (c. 165 B.C.). This persecution was especially violent, and the nation needed to hear God's word of hope.

Most chapters offer a separate exploit or vision. Chapter one, for example, tells how Daniel and three young Jews were taken into the household of the king and disobeyed his commands when they refused to eat unclean foods. Yet God protected them and made them prosper (Antiochus was trying to make Jews deny their faith by eating pork).

One of the dreams presented tells about a statue made of various elements. The feet of the statue were made of clay and iron, showing the instability of the regime of Antiochus.

Another dream—one had by King Nebuchadnezzar—tells how the king came to live like a beast for a certain period, for his use of power and his failure to recognize the power of God was beastlike.

Two of the most famous of the stories are those of the three young men being cast into the furnace and Daniel being thrown into the lions' den. In both of these stories the heroes refused to follow the command of the king not to worship Yahweh. The king tried to punish them, but God protected His beloved witnesses from harm.

Both of these stories were intended to encourage those called upon to give heroic witness during these persecutions.

Chapters 13 and 14 are a type of supplement to the book that presents the story of Susanna. It tells of a young woman, Susanna, wrongfully accused of adultery by two lecherous old men. Daniel, the man of great wisdom, saved her from death and brought the two false witnesses to judgment. God once again protected the innocent from the lies of evil ones.

This book is unlike earlier prophecies, for it is written in a new style: apocalyptic. This is why it contains so many strange dreams and visions, symbols and secret revelations. As already noted, the book of Revelation is also written in this style.

The book of Daniel can also be a consolation to us today, for even though we are not facing persecution, it can be difficult to find the courage to do God's will. Daniel encourages us, no matter what the cost, to bear witness to God's love.

# Esther — The Courageous Queen

*Esther 1—10*

IN times of crisis, people may be called upon to risk all (to become heroes) in order to protect those in danger. Esther, the heroine of the book bearing her name, is one such person.

The story of Esther takes place during the reign of King Ahasuerus of Persia (Xerxes, 485-465 B.C.). It opens with the king punishing the disobedience of his queen Vashti. When he searched for a replacement for her, a Hebrew girl, Hadasseh, was found and she entered his harem (receiving the Persian name Esther).

The king was so pleased with Esther that he made her his queen. Shortly afterward, Esther's uncle, Mordecai, discovered a plot against the king and revealed it to him through Esther.

Haman, the king's vizier, hated Mordecai, and resolved to have him and his people put to death. When the king issued the necessary edict, Mordecai told Esther to appeal to the King.

Esther was at first hesitant, given the danger in making such a request, but she then fasted and prayed and prepared herself. She invited the king and Haman to a banquet, and there she made her entreaty.

While the king was outside thinking, Haman threw himself at her feet asking for mercy. The king, entering at that moment, interpreted Haman's action as an attempt to seduce his queen, and he ordered him hung on the scaffold that Haman had prepared for Esther's uncle, Mordecai.

The last chapters of the book recount how the king issued an edict allowing the Jews to protect themselves by killing their enemies. To celebrate this change in fortune, Mordecai, the king's new vizier, sent letters to all the Jews telling them that they should celebrate a feast. The name of that feast is Purim (after the lot, or "Pur" that Haman had cast to pick the day of annihilation of the Jews).

There is considerable doubt that Esther is an historical figure. Some difficulties are: there is no record of a Queen Vashti or a Queen Esther in the Persian archives; according to the chronology of the book, Mordecai would have had to be at least 112 years old; and finally, it is highly unlikely that a Persian king would issue an edict allowing the Jews to kill their enemies.

The book was probably written in the second century B.C with a double intention: to justify the celebration of the feast of Purim and to show how God rescued His people from all their enemies (an important concern in times of persecution).

It reminds us today that we must trust in God to be with us in difficult times and also be willing to give our all when we are called upon to do so.

# Judith The Heroine

DURING times of oppression, it can be essential to tell stories of heroes so that one's own courage is fortified. This was the reason for the composition of the books of Daniel and Esther. The Jewish people were being persecuted by their Seleucid overlords. The very survival of the nation was at stake.

It might even be interpreted by some that God had abandoned His people. To combat that attitude, authors produced these books whose message was that God would defend those who were faithful to Him no matter how weak they were or how great the danger.

The book of Judith is another of these inspirational books produced during the second century B.C. The scene of the book is approximately 600 B.C., during the reign of Nebuchadnezzar, King of Babylon.

However, the author makes numerous historical errors. Because of these errors, it is obvious that the book was not written any time close to the Babylonian exile.

As a result of this and the various attitudes and themes found throughout the book, it is almost certain that Judith was written around the same time as Daniel and Esther and for the same reason as those books.

The plot of Judith involves an invasion by the Babylonian army. King Nebuchadnezzar sent his army to invade Judah under the command of his general, Holofernes. When Holofernes heard that the Judahites had prepared a defense against his army, he consulted local princes to determine how strong the Jews might be.

One of them, Achior, leader of the Ammonites, warned Holofernes that the Jews could be defeated only if they had sinned against their God. Holofernes ignored this warning and besieged the Jewish city of Bethulia.

The Babylonians cut off the water of the city so that many Judahites contemplated surrender. They were strongly opposed by a young widow, Judith, who urged her fellow citizens to trust in God.

Judith prayed to God, placing herself and her people in His care. She then went to the camp of Holofernes, feigning her approval of what he was doing and promising him victory. He was infatuated by her and invited her to a meal in his tent.

God protected her honor in the tent, for Holofernes passed out after becoming intoxicated. She then cut off his head and took it into Bethulia.

Achior, marveling at what God had done through Judith, was converted. The Jews of Bethulia then attacked the enemy camp, and they were totally victorious.

The moral of the story is that those who trust in the Lord will never be disappointed. God will answer their prayers (maybe not always in the way they hope, but always for their ultimate good).

# Mary    The Handmaid of the Lord

*Matthew 1—2; 12:46-50; 13:55; Mark 3:31-35; 6:3; Luke 1—2; 8:19-21; John 2:1-5; 19:25-27; Acts 1:14*

MARY was a simple girl from a small town—someone of whom few would take notice. Yet in that simplicity and lowliness, she represented an entire class of people in Israel: the Anawim, or poor of Yahweh.

These poor, uneducated people were despised by the rich and powerful, but because they had no pretentions and depended totally on God, they were beloved of the Lord.

It was for this reason (total trust in God) that Mary was chosen to be the mother of the Son of God.

The story of the birth of Jesus is told in the first two chapters of the books of Matthew and Luke.

An angel announced to Mary that she would bear a son. Not being married (for she was only engaged to Joseph), she was confused.

The angel explained to her that the Spirit of the Lord would work this marvel through her. Her response to this call was one of total acceptance, total willingness to serve the Lord.

Rather than becoming proud because of the great honor shown her, Mary's first thought was to serve others. She went to help her cousin Elizabeth, who was also pregnant.

When it came time for Mary to give birth, she and Joseph found themselves in Bethlehem (they had gone there for a census). She bore the child in a manger, for there was no room in the inns for them.

The first to honor her child were the simple people, the shepherds of Bethlehem. Next, three kings, pagans, came to honor him. At the child's circumcision, the aged Simeon directed to Mary words of joy and sorrow concerning Jesus.

The rich and powerful of her own land tried to kill the child (for their riches and power had blinded them to the ways of God). So Joseph took the family to Egypt for safety.

When all was clear, the holy family returned from Egypt and settled in Nazareth.

When Jesus was twelve, the holy family went to the temple at Jerusalem. Mary was accidentally separated from her Son for three days and finally found Him amid the doctors in the temple.

Mary is not mentioned often after these chapters.

She was at the wedding feast of Cana where she showed her faith in the power of her son.

Mary also visited Him once when Jesus told His disciples that the bonds of faith are more important than the bonds of blood.

This pronouncement certainly did not exclude Mary, for she was a woman of great faith. That faith is displayed by her heroic stance at the foot of the cross, watching her beloved son die.

That same faith received the seal of the Holy Spirit on Pentecost Day, for she was with the apostles in the upper room when the Holy Spirit descended upon them.

John the Apostle adopted Mary as his mother at the cross, and he cared for her for the rest of her life on earth (until she was taken body and soul into heaven).

# Joseph     Foster Father of Jesus

*Matthew 1—2; Luke 1—2*

JOSEPH was a simple, decent man who probably never dreamed that anything great could happen to him. He, in fact, did little more than one would expect any father to do, and yet in doing that he responded to God's call in a wondrous manner.

Joseph was a carpenter in the small town of Nazareth. He was betrothed to Mary, a girl from the same town. When word came to him that Mary was pregnant, he was perplexed. Technically, she could be condemned for being an adultress and stoned to death.

Being compassionate, Joseph decided to divorce her quietly and let it go at that. He had a dream, though, that changed his plans. An angel appeared to him and explained that Mary had conceived by the Holy Spirit. Accepting this revelation with full faith, he took Mary to himself.

When the Roman emperor ordered a census to be conducted, Joseph took his wife down to Bethlehem, his ancestral village (for he was of the house of David). There Mary gave birth to Jesus in a stable (for there was no room in the inn).

Shepherds from the neighboring fields came to adore him followed by three Magi who had traveled from afar.

However, the visit of the Magi endangered the life of Jesus, for through them King Herod heard of His birth and he sought to kill Him. Forewarned in a dream, Joseph took the child and His mother and fled to Egypt where he remained until Herod died. Afterward he returned to Nazareth.

We know Joseph was a religious man for he led his family in the fulfillment of the prescribed rites in the temple when Jesus was born.

Joseph took his family to Jerusalem when Jesus was twelve years old (the trip during which Jesus remained behind for three days and was finally found teaching the doctors of the temple).

After that incident, nothing more is heard of Joseph. It is presumed that he died sometime before Jesus began His public ministry.

It cannot be said, however, that Joseph's contribution to salvation history was inconsequential. He protected the child Messiah and taught Him his trade. He must have also taught Him some of his kindness and concern for the downtrodden.

Modern psychology tells us that so much of our personality is formed in our early years, and Joseph and Mary were around Jesus and taught Him in word and deed during those years of His life.

Joseph is a model for every father—a man of self-sacrifice, of concern. He didn't have to do great things to be great; he only had to be a loving father and husband.

# Jesus The Son of God

*Matthew, Mark, Luke, John*

IN the Old Testament, there are not many instances when human beings met God face to face. One of the most memorable was when Elijah was on the holy mountain and he awaited God's presence.

The prophet saw a hurricane, earthquake, and fire, but God was not present in any of them. Then he heard a gentle wind, and God was present in that breeze.

This appearance of God serves as a parable to understand better God's appearance as man in the person of Jesus. For hundreds of years the Jewish people had awaited a Messiah of power, one who would help them destroy their enemies. They awaited a warrior Messiah, a kingly Messiah who would rule over all.

When Jesus finally appeared, He deeply shocked them. He was not the warrior or the king as they expected Him to be. Rather He was that gentle breeze.

Jesus spoke of love and not vengeance. He became a servant rather than a ruler. He completely emptied Himself rather than demanding honor.

As Jesus preached His message of reconciliation with God and among humans, He deeply offended those who had other expectations. To those who awaited a political solution to the problems of the Jewish people, He said that it was not really important who ruled their land as long as they served God.

There were those who were devoted to the law, but Jesus relativized its value telling them that the law was made for humans and not humans for the law.

Those who wanted ritual purity were offended when He ate with public sinners.

Jesus even offended His fellow citizens of Nazareth for they knew Him as He grew up, and they could not picture Him as being the Messiah.

Most of all, Jesus scandalized and astounded all Jews by intimating that He was one with God the Father.

To all of those who would listen to His message, Jesus offered new life. He spoke of being reborn in the Spirit of God so that we would no longer live for ourselves or the world but would live for God instead. He healed, forgave, even raised people from the dead.

For all this good that Jesus did, His own people had a hand in putting Him to death. Yet He would not allow this act of hate to defeat Him.

By His death on the cross Jesus defeated sin, and by being risen from the dead He defeated even death. With His death and resurrection He reversed the values of the world so that we could choose to die to ourselves to live with Him.

Most of all, Jesus promised that we would never be alone. He is with us until He returns in glory at the end of time.

# John The Baptist

*Gospels; Acts 13:24f; 18:25; 19:3*

IT CAN be difficult for someone who is always in the background, someone who does the difficult work while another gets the credit. Yet, if we recognized our proper role, then it is not really important whether or not we get the credit. All that is important is that each person follows God as he or she is called.

John the Baptist fully recognized his role in relation to Jesus. He was the precursor while Jesus was the Messiah. He was to diminish, Jesus to increase. He was the best man, and Jesus was the bridegroom.

John's very first act recorded in the Bible was to move in the womb of his mother, Elizabeth, paying homage to the child Jesus who was in Mary's womb.

John's life was spent preparing the way for the Messiah. He preached conversion from sinful ways. He baptized those who listened with a baptism of conversion. By doing this, he removed the obstacles that would keep them from recognizing Jesus when He came.

Like Jesus, John preached to sinners, to those who had been rejected by the Jewish hierarchy. His greatest successes were among tax collectors and public sinners.

Those who should have been the first to recognize him, the so-called religious ones of the land, were unmoved by his words. John was scathing in his attacks on them, calling them a race of vipers.

Ironically, while sinners were able to remove the obstacles that would prevent them from recognizing Jesus, those who thought that they were righteous could not. They had come to depend upon their own strengths and did not know how to depend on God.

Much of what John taught was similar to what the Essenes were also teaching. The Essenes were a community of monks who lived near the Dead Sea and who preached a life of preparation for the coming battle between the forces of light and those of darkness.

John baptized not far from where they lived, and he might even have been in contact with them.

The climax of John's mission came the day that Jesus approached him to be baptized. Although John tried to refuse for he realized that he was unworthy to baptize Jesus, yet Jesus insisted.

From that moment it was Jesus who was the center of attention while John, having completed his mission, faded into the background.

Shortly after this, John was arrested by King Herod Antipas. He had denounced the immoral marriage of Herod to his brother's wife. Herod feared John and recognized him to be a man of God. He feared John too much to have him killed, but Salome, the daughter of his wife, tricked him into having John beheaded.

# Peter     The Rock

*Gospels; Acts 1—12; 1 Corinthians 1:12; 3: 22; 9:5; 15:5; Galatians 1—2; 1 and 2 Peter*

WHEN Jesus calls each of us to follow Him, He invites us with all of our strengths and weaknesses. He asks us to put our strengths at the service of the Good News and to trust in Him that His power might shine through our weaknesses.

Interestingly enough, the former is often easier to do than the latter. It is easy to trust in God and serve Him when we are in charge—it is not so easy when we realize our unworthiness.

Peter, the apostle, came to a painful realization of this in his own life. A fisherman when called (like his brother Andrew), Peter was promised by Jesus that he would become a fisher of human beings.

Peter was one of the first called, and right from the beginning he seems to have occupied a prominent position among the apostles. In many of the Gospel stories that deal with the apostles, Peter is their spokesman. He is, for example, the apostle who asks Jesus how often one must forgive a brother (and Jesus answers him seventy times seven).

Peter's readiness to speak up often borders on the impetuous. When Jesus asks the apostles who they believe Him to be, Peter responds that He is the Messiah. Likewise, when the apostles see Jesus walking on the water of the Sea of Galilee, it is Peter who gets out of the boat to come to Him.

However, both of these manifestations of faith all but end disastrously, for in both incidents Peter's faith is found to be lacking. In the former, Peter rebukes Jesus who announces that the Messiah must suffer; in the latter his faith wavers, and he begins to sink beneath the waves.

Likewise, Peter is quick to profess his allegiance to Christ at the Last Supper. Jesus, however, knows his weakness (even if Peter can't yet admit it).

When asked by Jesus to keep vigil with Him, Peter and the other disciples repeatedly fall asleep. Then, when Jesus is arrested, Peter denies knowing Jesus three times.

In spite of this tremendous failure, Peter is one of the first of the disciples to whom Jesus appears after the resurrection. According to the gospel of John, this was also the moment in which Jesus asked Peter three times if he loved Him.

In asking this, Jesus was entrusting to Peter the care of His flock. Peter would be the rock on which Jesus would build His Church.

The triple request served as a reminder to Peter of his triple denial. Peter, who failed when relying on his own strength, would be a rock inasmuch as he trusted in God's strength.

It was that trust that would allow Peter to live and to die for Christ.

# John The Beloved Disciple

*Throughout the New Testament*

WE know that God loves each of us individually, but sometimes we forget that this also means that He loves each of us in a different manner. It is not so much that He loves one and hates another, but more that His love will be expressed in one way for one and in quite another for the other person.

We must remember this when we speak about John the apostle. John calls himself the beloved disciple in his gospel. It is obvious when one reads that gospel that he was very close to the Lord.

All throughout John's following of Jesus he was singled out to be one of a central group who seemed to have been more important than the others: Peter, James, and John.

When Jesus was dying, He even entrusted His mother into John's care. After the ascension, John the apostle is reported to be one of the heads of the Church in Jerusalem.

Yet, despite it all, we cannot really say that God was playing favorites. Rather, the love with which He loved John was expressed in a very open manner because that is the type of expression that John needed in order to respond faithfully to his call.

What was the special duty to which John was called? It seems that he was called to express the theology of love which is found in the Johannine writings (the gospel of John, the letters of John and the book of Revelation; while John might not have written all of these, his theology is found in all of them).

Some of the things that are emphasized in Johannine theology are the need to have faith in Jesus, the life that Jesus brings us, and the importance of the sacraments (especially Baptism and the Eucharist) in sharing the life of God.

Jesus, for John, is a light come into a world filled with darkness. Humankind is trapped in that darkness of sin, but Jesus offers to liberate all who will accept His message. Humankind is given a choice: life or death.

It is not that God would annihilate the world if it didn't accept Jesus. He wouldn't even have to do that. If the world did not accept Jesus, it would already be spiritually dead.

It seems as if John wrote most of the works attributed to him toward the end of his life. The gospel of John, for example, was written quite a bit after the other three gospels had been written.

According to tradition, John is the only apostle not to have been martyred. During the persecutions he was exiled to the island of Patmos. He is said to be buried near there, in the vicinity of the city of Ephesus.

# James    The Greater

*Matthew; Mark; Luke; Acts 1:13; 12:2*

ONE of the most highly prized values of this world is power. People want to obtain and exercise dominion over others. They feel self-worth in the measure in which they can control others.

It is difficult to maintain an equilibrium when the world preaches this message of exploitation. This is true today, and it was true in the days of Jesus.

Yet Jesus taught His disciples that they must adopt a new set of values. Their primary concern could not be in accruing power, but rather in service.

This message can be read in the story of James the Greater. James was the brother of John, son of Zebedee, and a fisherman like his brother, Peter, and Andrew. He was one of the first of the apostles to be called, and he seems to have occupied a privileged position among the apostles.

Three different times during the ministry Jesus limited the number of the disciples that He wanted to be with Him for an important event: when He healed the daughter of Jairus, at the Transfiguration, and during the agony in the garden. All three times He took only Peter, John, and James along with Him.

Because James was one of the early apostles and because he seems to have been closer to Jesus than most of the other apostles, it was natural for him to consider himself more powerful than the others. On two occasions he tried to exercise the power that he thought was his.

Once, when Jesus was on the way to Jerusalem with his disciples and they passed through a Samaritan town, the Samaritans refused to welcome them because He was heading toward Jerusalem. James and his brother John asked Jesus if they should call fire down upon the town like Sodom and Gomorrah to punish it. They wanted to use their supernatural power, and Jesus reproached them for their presumption.

On another occasion, the mother of James and John asked that her sons be given a privileged position in the kingdom of Jesus. Jesus asked them if they could drink of the chalice from which He was about to drink, and they said that they could. Jesus then told them that although they would drink of that chalice, it was not His to give them positions of honor.

By asking him to drink of the chalice, Jesus was telling James that he would have to lay down his life in imitation of his Master. James was not to exercise his apostleship by grasping for power, but by emptying himself out in self-sacrificing love.

This call to radical witness on the part of James was soon realized, for in 42 A.D. he was killed by Herod Agrippa I and became one of the first martyrs of the Church.

# Andrew The Fisherman

*Matthew 10:2-4; 16:17; Mark 1:16-20. 29; 3:16ff; 13:3; Luke 5:10; 6:14ff;*
*John 1:35ff; 6:5-9; 12:20-22; Acts 1:13*

ALTHOUGH Andrew is the brother of Peter and considered to be one of the founders of the Church in the East (Turkey, Greece, etc.), there is not much written about him in the Bible. He is listed along with the other apostles in the various lists of apostles.

Beside that, Andrew is also mentioned in two incidents along with Philip the apostle. The first of these incidents is the multiplication of loaves and fishes as reported in the gospel of John. Andrew reports to Jesus, "There is a lad here who has five barley loaves and a couple of dried fish, but what good is that for so many?"

In the other episode, a group of Greeks had asked Philip to introduce them to Jesus, and Andrew served along with Philip as their intermediary.

More telling are the two accounts of Andrew's calling by Jesus. In the account found in the gospel of John, Andrew is mentioned as being one of John the Baptist's disciples. As he and another disciple were walking with John, he pointed to Jesus and announced, "Look: There is the Lamb of God."

Those two disciples followed Jesus and observed what He was doing. Andrew was so impressed that he went to call his brother, Peter, telling him, "We have found the Messiah!"

In the synoptic account, Andrew is called along with Peter while they were fishing in their father's boat. Jesus told them that He would make them fishers of humans, and they left their father's boat and followed Him.

Both of the accounts are probably true. Andrew might have come to know Jesus when he was following John, and only later did he actually begin to follow Jesus as a disciple.

Andrew was in a unique position to be able to contrast the apostolate of John the Baptist with that of Jesus. John's was an apostolate of conversion to prepare the people for the coming Messiah. It was a question of removing obstacles. His baptism was to wash one free from sins.

The baptism and apostolate of Jesus had a different intention. His baptism was only partially one of repentance—it was also one of new life, of union with God.

Jesus' preaching, likewise, was concerned with union with God. He spoke of what it meant to be a child of God. He invited all to consider God as being their father. Even the title that John the Baptist used for Jesus, Lamb of God, points to that new rapport between God and human beings, for He was the lamb of the new covenant.

That message is essential for Christians today. All too often their Christianity consists in doing things or not doing things (not unlike the message of John). Like Andrew, we must pass beyond that and come to know God one on one.

# Philip     A Man of Faith and Failures

*Matthew 10:3; Mark 3:18; Luke 6:14; John 1:43-48; 6:5-7; 12:21f; 14:8; Acts 1:13*

THERE are some who find it easy to place their trust in God. Once they have decided that they will follow Him, all else follows naturally. It is almost as if the hand of God shelters them from doubt and confusion.

There are others, however, who must struggle with their faith. Their faith-life seems to be a series of ever higher plateaus unto which they must climb.

Most of us fall somewhere in the middle between these two extremes. At times we seem to be ready to dedicate our lives totally to God, while at others we are barely able to follow His call.

Philip, the apostle, seems to follow the third of these patterns. At times he is a paragon of faith; at others his response to the promptings of Jesus is woefully inadequate.

The synoptic gospels speak very little about Philip, mentioning him only in the list of the apostles. John, however, mentions him in four different places. The first, 1:43-48, is the call of Philip by Jesus.

We are told simply that Philip was from the same town as Peter and Andrew, Bethsaida, and Jesus called him with the words, "Follow Me."

Although the sacred text doesn't actually say so, it is obvious that Philip responded well to the call, for he immediately went and called Nathanael to meet Jesus, whom he believed to be the Messiah.

Philip is next seen in chapter 6 when Jesus asked Philip where they might buy enough bread to feed the crowd of people listening to the teachings of Jesus. The text says specifically that Jesus asked Philip this to test him.

Philip seems to have failed the test, for his answer shows that he is thinking in a purely material sense and doesn't consider the power of Jesus over all creation, as seen when He then multiplied the bread to feed the people.

In chapter 12 Philip once again appears to be a man of faith. He serves as a intermediary for some Greeks who wanted to meet Jesus.

Then in chapter 14 he is once again the man of inadequate faith. He asks Jesus to show him the Father and earns the Master's reproof, "Philip, after I have been with you all this time, you still do not know Me? Whoever has seen Me has seen the Father. How can you say, 'Show us the Father'?"

Tradition holds that Philip preached the Good News in Turkey and there was martyred for the faith.

Thus, the faith and even the failures of Philip are a great consolation to us. They show us someone much like ourselves, one who tries, fails, but gets up again. Like him, we must allow our faith to grow by trusting in the love and mercy of God.

# Thomas   The Doubter

*Matthew 10:2-4; Mark 3:16-19; Luke 6:14-16; John 11:16; 14:5; 20:24-29; 21:2; Acts 1:13*

FAITH is not a prepackaged reality that each person can acquire at a given price. Rather, it is a personal gift from God to an individual. Each person receives it in a different manner and at a different time. For some, the ride is easy, for others it is a tremendous struggle.

The twelve apostles of Jesus illustrate this point. Each had his own calling, and each responded in his own way. Some were generous, others impetuous, some hesitant and doubting, and one failed completely.

Thomas is traditionally designated as the apostle whose faith was not a ready faith, one who doubted in the veracity of the resurrection.

Thomas is not mentioned very often in the Gospels. In the synoptic gospels he is mentioned only in the lists of apostles. He appears four times in the gospel of John.

In his debut, 11:16, Thomas urges his fellow apostles to accompany Jesus to Jerusalem that they might die with Him. The verse suggests a certain impetuous nature, but also one that is generous. He realizes that there is danger in following Jesus, and he is willing to put his life on the line.

What Thomas does not yet comprehend is the reason why one should lay down his life for Jesus. His loyalty is a human loyalty to a beloved teacher—only later would it be loyalty to his Lord and God.

Thomas' misreading of Jesus' intentions can be observed in 14:5. Jesus had just told His apostles that He would go to the Father and they would follow Him. Thomas asked Jesus how they could follow Him if they did not know where He was going.

That is exactly the problem—he didn't know where Jesus was going. Although he was willing to die for Jesus, he didn't yet understand what it meant to live for Jesus.

This lack of comprehension is again seen after the resurrection. When Jesus appeared to His apostles the night of the resurrection, Thomas was not with them. They recounted to him what they had seen and heard, but he could not believe them.

The next Sunday, Jesus appeared again to the apostles. He offered to Thomas the possibility to do what he had demanded—to touch the wounds of His passion. Thomas had wanted to do this to be sure that this was the same Jesus he had known before the cross. Thomas responded to this offer by professing his faith, "My Lord and my God."

Finally Thomas understood the significance of what it meant to live for Christ and to die for Christ. It was a struggle, but his faith was finally mature. He calls to us who have not seen the risen Christ to believe, to live and die for Christ.

# Bartholomew    The True Israelite

*Matthew 10:3; Mark 3:18; Luke 6:14; Acts 1:13; John 1:45-51; 21:2*

BARTHOLOMEW, the apostle, is a man of mystery. The only place that his name is mentioned in the Bible is in the list of the twelve apostles. We are not even sure that Bartholomew is his real name, for it could easily be his "surname," meaning the "son of Talmai."

If Bartholomew is not his name, we should be curious about what his name is. Scholars who have studied this question have suggested that the Bartholomew in Matthew, Mark, and Luke is the same man as the Nathanael mentioned in John. The reason for this is that Bartholomew is listed in connection with Philip in Matthew, Mark, and Luke while Nathanael is connected with Philip in John.

Bartholomew is not mentioned at all in John's gospel (which we would expect if John were calling him Nathanael), and Nathanael, who is mentioned together with the prominent apostles in John, is not even mentioned in the other Gospels (which again would be the case if they were calling him Bartholomew).

Nathanael's (Bartholomew's) most important appearance in the gospel of John is in chapter 1:45-51. Philip had just been called by Jesus and had followed Him. Believing in Jesus, Philip wanted to share his faith with his friends. He went to Nathanael and told him, "We have found the one Moses spoke of in the law—the prophets too—Jesus, son of Joseph from Nazareth."

Nathanael was skeptical for Nazareth was a dirt poor town, and he doubted that the Messiah could come from there. Nevertheless he followed Philip and met Jesus.

When Jesus saw Nathanael, He said, "This man is a true Israelite; there is no guile in him." This was a word play, for the name Jacob can mean "guile."

Jacob's other name (given to him when he wrestled with God) was Israel. Thus, this was a man who was like Israel (who had encountered God) and not like Jacob (who based his life on trickery).

Jesus then told Nathanael that He saw him under the fig tree. We do not know if he had been praying there or dreaming, but whatever Nathanael had been doing, it was a sign to him that Jesus was in fact the Messiah.

Nathanael professed his faith in Jesus, and Jesus assured him that he would see greater things—angels ascending and descending on the Son of Man (another of Jacob's visions).

Tradition holds that Bartholomew preached in India, Armenia, and other eastern countries and he died a martyr.

His encounter with Jesus reminds us that at a certain point in our lives we must stop playing games (the guile of Jacob) and open ourselves in honesty to God's presence in our lives (to be true Israelites).

# Matthew — The Tax Collector

*Matthew 9:9ff; 10:3; Mark 2:14ff; 3:8; Luke 5:27-29; 6:15; Acts 1:13*

WE know that sin separates us from the love of God, so it only seems obvious that if we were great sinners, God would want nothing to do with us. This was the message that the Pharisees and the other leaders of the Jews found in the Old Testament. They treated sinners as outcasts—people who were to be avoided at all costs.

Jesus not only showed hesitancy in accepting this conclusion; He actually taught that the opposite was true. He called Himself a doctor who had come to heal those wounded by sin. He associated with the outcasts of His society: prostitutes, infamous sinners, and the like so that they might have the Good News and be saved.

Matthew, the evangelist, was one of those wounded people whom Jesus called. Matthew, also known as Levi, was a tax collector. Those who performed that task were hated by the Jews.

They were viewed as being collaborators with the occupying power: Rome. For this reason, devout Jews would never consider this occupation, nor would they associate with those who were engaged in it.

Jesus' call of Matthew was a simple message, "Follow Me." Matthew's response was equally simple, for he, "got up and followed Him." The importance of that simple call, though, should not be missed.

Before the call, Matthew was dead—dead to sin, dead and impure to those around him. After the call Matthew was healed—both from his sin and from those divisions between people that are created by sin.

This is exemplified by the fact that Jesus went to his house and shared in a banquet offered by Matthew. The other guests of the banquet were tax collectors and public sinners.

The Pharisees were scandalized by the fact that Jesus would eat with them, but Jesus rebuked their self-righteous stance and assured them that His message was addressed precisely to these sinners. They, at least, realized that they needed God's healing love, while the Pharisees believed that they had already earned their own salvation.

This call from death to life helped shape the way Matthew wrote his gospel. He proclaims the message that Jesus was promulgating a new law—one of love and healing, and not the law of death like that promulgated by Moses. He had seen clearly that the self-righteousness of the Pharisees had led to hate, while the forgiveness of Jesus culminated in new life.

This message is a powerful reminder to us. We can never forget that we are sinners and in desperate need of God's healing (lest we become self-righteous like the Pharisees). We can also never forget that no matter how terribly we have sinned, God wants us to turn back to Him and to be forgiven.

# James   The Lesser

*Mathew 10:3; 13:55; 27:56; Mark 3:18; 6:3; 15:40; 16:1; Luke 6:15; Acts 1:13; 12:17; 15:13-23; 21:8; 1 Corinthians 15:7; Galatians 2:12*

IT is a bit difficult to identify with precision who James the Lesser might be. This is true because there are a number of different individuals in the New Testament with the name of James.

One, James the Greater, is the son of Zebedee and the brother of John. Another is James, the father of Judas.

There is also a James, the son of Alphaeus, who is mentioned as being an apostle.

There is James, one of the brethren of the Lord and brother of Joseph (or Joses), Simon, and Jude.

Finally, there is a certain James, the son of Mary. (This Mary is one of the women who witnessed the crucifixion.)

Many scholars believe that the last three men named above are the same person. James, whose father's name was Alphaeus and whose mother's name was Mary, was also the brother of Joseph, Simon, and Jude.

This James was a relative of Jesus, probably his cousin. He was called by Jesus to follow Him as an apostle, and after the ascension he served as one of the leaders of the Jewish Christian community in Jerusalem (along with Peter and John).

Some non-Catholic scholars do not agree with that identification. They have two arguments for challenging it.

First of all, they feel that when the Gospels speak of the "brothers of Jesus," they are speaking about actual brothers. This would mean that James (according to them) would be the younger brother of Jesus (whose parents would be Joseph and Mary).

Also, they argue that the Gospels generally report the family of Jesus as being hostile to His ministry, so that it would be unlikely that one of His relatives would have been an apostle.

The Catholic Church has always maintained that Jesus was an only child. This is a tradition that was strong even in the earliest days of the Church. It explains the "brothers of Jesus" phrase as referring not to His blood brothers, but rather to His relatives, a valid translation of the word used in the Gospels.

Concerning the second objection, it is not entirely true that members of the family of Jesus were really hostile—it would be fairer to say that they were confused over the role of Jesus.

But even if Jesus' relatives were confused, it doesn't automatically preclude one of their members from becoming an apostle (for even the apostles were confused for quite some time over the role of Jesus).

Knowing Jesus as closely as James did, he had a special difficulty in recognizing Jesus as the Son of God. He had to look beyond the appearances and see his cousin with the eyes of faith (something that we must do with those who surround us).

— 123 —

# Simon    The Zealot

*Matthew 10:4; Mark 3:18; Luke 6:15; Acts 1:13*

EACH one of us has a different idea of how God should become involved in our lives. Some would prefer that He be much more manifest; others would prefer that He leave us alone.

Most of us, however, believe that God should not allow the wicked to get their way quite as often as they do. He should reward the good for their faithfulness and punish the wicked even now.

This was the approach of the Jewish people at the time of Jesus. They were a people who had suffered greatly throughout their history, and at the time of Jesus they were under the heel of the Roman conquerer.

Accordingly, the Jewish people believed that since they had been faithful to God and the Romans were faithless pagans, God should help them to gain their independence from Rome.

There was a group of Jews who spearheaded the quest for independence from the Romans: the Zealots. Their name is derived from the word "zeal," for they were zealots for the ways of the Lord.

The Zealots rejected any compromise with the enemy, and at times they formed terrorist units to do battle with Rome.

They, like other Jews, expected God to send them a Messiah. Their idea of Messiah was a political and military leader like David or Judas Maccabee who would defeat all the enemies of Israel.

When Jesus began to preach His Good News, He attracted the attention of both religious and political leaders. The Zealots thought of Him as being a prime candidate for Messiah. A number of times it seemed as if the crowd would carry Jesus off and proclaim Him to be king.

Simon, the Zealot, came to Jesus with these expectations. He was a good and faithful Israelite who wanted nothing else than that the power of God be seen on the earth. To follow Jesus, though, he had to abandon his ideas of what the Messiah would be.

Jesus rejected the notion that He should be a revolutionary leader. His kingdom was not of this world.

Jesus had come to change our hearts, and not to change political systems. He called us to love and not to rebellion.

Jesus called us to surrender to the will of God, even if that means that we would have to suffer for now under the oppression of evil.

Like Simon, we must lay aside our preconceptions of the way that God should act toward us. Rather than trying to control His hand, we must accept what God wants for us.

We must live in the world, but not be of this world. This doesn't mean that we should be indifferent to injustice, but rather that we should change the world by first converting our own hearts.

# Jude Thaddeus     Patron of Hopeless Causes

*Matthew 10:3; 13:55; Mark 3:18; 6:3; Luke 6:16; Acts 1:13; Letter of Jude*

WHEN we speak of the communion of saints, we mean our union with those who followed God during their lives and are now sharing in the eternal life of God. These are individuals who have run the good race and who have reached their goal.

Sometimes, though, we talk about them as if they are in some never-never land. We forget that while they have finished their own race, they are still involved in our race.

Being one with the love that is God, they want to share that love with those in need. Therefore, they guide us, educate us, intercede for us, serve as our models, and in many other ways express their love for us.

Jude Thaddeus is a tremendous example of an individual who served the Lord while alive on earth and who still serves Him and us in the communion of saints. Jude (or Judas) was one of the apostles called by Jesus.

We know very, very little about his apostolate, for concerning that we only have his name on a list of apostles. We also believe that he is the same Jude mentioned as being a cousin of Jesus.

There are some scholars who doubt this identification. They believe that the Gospels imply that most of the relatives of Jesus were critical of His mission. Thus, they argue, it would be unlikely for one of the cousins of Jesus to become an apostle (the same argument is used in connection with James the Lesser).

The argument, however, is not overwhelming. Although the Gospels do imply that the relatives of Jesus were skeptical of the mission of Jesus, they do not state that all of them were hostile. It is possible that some accepted Him and even became His apostles.

Since the argument against Jude being the cousin of Jesus is not very strong, and tradition dating back to the early church favors his kinship to Jesus, we should probably hold that position.

Beside this tentative identification and the fact that he was an apostle, we know nothing else from scripture about Jude. Tradition holds that he was a missionary in the countries of the East and died a martyr there.

Jude is, in certain ways, possibly more important to us after his death than before. St. Jude is known as the patron of hopeless causes (especially in Anglo-Saxon countries). He is an example of one of the saints who expressed his love for us during his ministry on earth (he gave his life for the Gospel) and after his death by his continuing concern or intervention for us.

When people ask for his intercession, they are asking not so much that he do something. Rather they are asking that he once again be a vehicle of God's love (for whether on earth or in heaven, all that he accomplished is done through the Lord.)

# Judas Iscariot   The Traitor

*Matthew 10:4; 26; 27; Mark 3:19; 14; Luke 6:16; 22; John 6:71; 12:4-6; 13:21-26; Acts 1:18*

WHY would a person do such a terrible thing? No matter how much we meditate on it, that question always returns to us. How could someone have betrayed our Lord Jesus? Why did Judas do it?

To that question, we have few indications that would help us arrive at a conclusion. The evangelists who wrote about Judas and his betrayal tend to draw the picture in harsh tones—for them Judas was a liar and a thief. He betrayed Jesus for the basest of motives: money.

Yet we have to ask whether their reports are entirely objective. Could their evaluation of the personality of Judas be an over-simplification based on their revulsion for the man who betrayed their Lord? Is it possible that Judas had other motives, motives that might even be considered to be more honorable (certainly they were mistaken, but maybe not as petty as the Gospels report).

Certainly the fact that Jesus chose him as an apostle would seem to point to the fact that he was not entirely despicable (unless, of course, one believes that Jesus chose him only so that there would be someone to betray Him and thus fulfill what had been predicted—but that would seem somewhat utilitarian on the part of Jesus).

What, then, could these motives have been? It is at this point that we must resort to speculation. Could it have been that Judas at first believed that Jesus was the Messiah, but then slowly became disillusioned with Him because He was not the type of Messiah for which he had been waiting? (It might be that, like the Zealots, he was waiting for a political Messiah who would throw off the yoke of Roman oppression.)

Could Judas have been confused about Jesus' habit of associating with known sinners and His apparent disregard for the prescriptions of the law? Is it possible that he just believed that Jesus was a false Messiah and had to be opposed?

Or is it even possible that Judas was acting to force the hand of Jesus—he wanted to put Him in a desperate situation so that Jesus would have to manifest His power and be proclaimed Messiah by the people.

This is, of course, all speculation, but it does raise an interesting possibility: that Judas thought he was serving God by betraying Jesus. That chilling possibility shows us the tremendous importance of purifying the motives for which we do things.

We must pray continuously; we must confront ourselves with the word of God as presented by the scriptures and by our brothers and sisters in the faith.

We cannot proceed blindly on our own prejudices and preconceived opinions. Rather we must be open to the action of God no matter how He presents Himself to us—for this is exactly what Judas failed to do!

# Matthias  The Replacement

*Acts 1:13-26*

IT is difficult for us to understand the importance of numbers in the Bible. Other than a couple of numbers that carry a special significance (e.g., seven or thirteen), they don't mean much to us.

That is not true of the Mid-Eastern culture in which the Bible was written. There numbers became a type of shorthand to express concepts.

The number seven, for example meant fullness. The number six, one less than seven, expressed a certain greatness that, nevertheless, fell short of the completeness of a seven. The number one thousand expressed an immensity.

This is why the fact that Jesus chose twelve apostles for Himself was not accidental. He chose twelve because it matched the number of the tribes of Israel.

Jesus intended to show that His group of men was like the patriarchs of the old Israel. Now there were twelve new patriarchs, and they would be the founders of a new Israel.

Again, this fact should not be underestimated. Some of the Jews were saying that Jesus was a heretic and a blasphemer. They claimed that He had no part in the traditions of the Jewish people.

Jesus, by choosing twelve new patriarchs, was responding to their accusations by stating that it was the accusers who were the ones unfaithful to the traditions of Israel. His followers were the true Israel, while those who did not follow Him were the Israel that had strayed away.

This whole dynamic explains why it was so important that the apostles choose a replacement for Judas when he killed himself. They desperately needed to conserve this symbolic message so that they could answer the charges of the hostile Jews.

Yet, the apostles felt themselves unworthy to choose a new apostle on their own authority. They realized, after all, that it was not they who had chosen to be apostles, but Christ who had chosen them. Therefore, they placed the matter in Christ's hands once again.

They established the criterion that an apostle be one who had followed Jesus from the day of His baptism till His ascension. There were two disciples who fit the description, so they prayed and drew lots. The lot fell to Matthias who thus became the twelfth apostle.

Very little is known about Matthias. His election as apostle is the only time that his name is mentioned in the Bible. Tradition holds that he ministered in Asia Minor and was martyred near the Caspian Sea.

Matthias' choice, though, teaches us about the plan of God. It reminds us of God's loving concern. He loves us so much that He would let no obstacle, even betrayal by one of His chosen ones, interfere in the establishment of the New Israel.

# Mary Magdalene    The Grateful Lover

*Matthew 27:56, 61; 28:1-10; Mark 15:40, 47; 16:1-9; Luke 8:2; 24:10; John 19:25; 20:1-18*

IF one of us were to have an incurable illness and every doctor to whom we went would give an equally pessimistic evaluation, and then we were to go to one doctor who not only offered us hope but actually cured us, we would be extremely grateful to that doctor.

We would praise him and try to make him famous. We would want all those who were afflicted as we had been to hear of him and be healed as we were.

This is exactly what happened to Mary Magdalene. (Mary should not be confused with either Mary, sister of Martha, or the woman who was caught in adultery.) Mary had been possessed by seven demons, and Jesus freed her from this malady.

She was incredibly grateful to Him for this, and she resolved to spend her life in His service. She is listed as one of the women who followed Jesus and His apostles and ministered to their needs.

Even more telling than this is the fact that Mary Magdalene is one of the few people listed as being at the foot of the cross. She was risking her life by being there, but it did not matter to her.

Jesus had given her the true life of faith when He had healed her. That was all that mattered to her anymore.

It was that faith and devotion to Jesus which brought her to the tomb on that first Easter morning. She had gone there to anoint Jesus' body, but she did not find Him there. Instead an angel announced to her that Jesus had been raised from the dead and entrusted her to carry that message to the disciples.

In John's gospel, the account is a bit more stylized (the language is based upon the poetry of the Song of Songs). In that account, Mary is seen as a symbol of the Church which goes searching for its Lord.

Like the Church, Mary had been called from the death of sin to new life in Jesus. Mary, in that account, attempts to embrace her risen Lord, but she is told not to do so, for she, like the Church, could no longer possess the bodily Jesus.

Rather than clinging to what was material, Mary is told to proclaim the resurrection to the disciples (just as the Church must courageously proclaim that message).

We are all like Mary Magdalene, for we have all been healed of the demons that held us prisoners. We have all been given new life—and called to live totally for and with Jesus.

Our lives must be spent in witness to His death (by dying to ourselves) so that we might be witnesses to His resurrection.

# Martha and Mary    Friends of the Lord

*Luke 10:38-42; John 11; 12:3-8*

IT is strange how two brothers or two sisters can often be a as different from each other as night and day. That is true of Martha and Mary. The gospels of Luke and John used their differences to offer us a lesson.

Martha and Mary lived in the village of Bethany, not far from Jerusalem. They seem to have been at least moderately wealthy (at least rich enough to be able to host Jesus and His disciples). They lived with their brother, Lazarus, and their family was close to Jesus.

The most famous incident reported in the Gospels involving Martha and Mary took place at a dinner which they were holding for Jesus. Once Jesus had been invited to their house, there was much work to do to prepare the meal.

Martha busied herself with that work. Her sister, Mary, surprisingly did not help her at all with the preparations. Rather, she sat down and listened to the teachings of Jesus.

Martha went up to Jesus and asked Him to tell Mary that she should be helping her sister. Jesus refused to do that, and rather told Martha that Mary had chosen the better portion.

Most commentators who have reflected on these verses have suggested that Jesus was telling them that it was better to busy oneself with the things of God rather than human concerns. Thus, Jesus was applauding Mary who had a spirit of contemplation and not approving of Martha who did not.

There is another possible interpretation to this same story. Rather than being a choice between contemplation and its lack, it could also be interpreted as a choice between people-oriented people and task-oriented people. Martha was so busy with the things that she was doing that she forgot to host the people that she had before her.

These two interpretations are not irreconcilable. Many people today treat God as if He were a thing (a theory or force) rather than a person. Religious activity is conducted in the same spirit as watching TV—"it is a nice story, but . . ." It is seen as something that we must do, an obligation, but not as something that involves a loving commitment.

In allowing that type of attitude, one falls into the "Martha syndrome" in both respects, for one is neither contemplative nor is one loving a person.

This story should challenge us to ask ourselves, "Who is God for me? Do I really know Him at all? How can I come to know Him better?"

The only other incident in the Bible involving both sisters is the resurrection of Lazarus, their brother, from the dead (seen under Lazarus).

# Lazarus     The Resurrected

*John 11—12*

LAZARUS and his two sisters, Martha and Mary, were close friends of Jesus. They probably hosted Him at their house a number of times. Because they were His friends, it was only natural that He would do a favor or two for them.

Yet what Jesus did for them could never be described as simply being a favor done for a friend. He gave them life itself (in both a figurative and a literal sense).

Lazarus and his sisters lived in Bethany, a town not far from Jerusalem. One day Lazarus became very ill, and his sisters sent for Jesus so that He might be with them. They firmly believed that if He were there, then nothing evil would happen to their brother.

Jesus, who was across the Jordan, did not return immediately. When He finally did arrive in Bethany, it was too late (or so it seemed), for Lazarus was dead.

When Jesus arrived, Martha ran out to meet Him. She told Jesus that if He had been there, she was sure that her brother wouldn't have died. Jesus answered her that even now it was not too late, for He was the resurrection and the life.

Mary likewise told Jesus that she was sure that Lazarus would still be alive if He had been present. (One wonders if this wasn't an implicit complaint for Jesus' failure to return as soon as He heard of the illness.)

Jesus went to the tomb and wept bitterly. It is important to note that Jesus does not give a half-hearted reaction to death—He views it as something that is evil and about which He weeps.

Jesus would be surprised if we did not feel the pain of separation and react accordingly. He only asks that we ultimately trust in Him.

Jesus then ordered that the stone covering the tomb be removed. Martha tried to convince Him not to do this for the body was already decomposing, but He insisted.

When the tomb was opened Jesus ordered Lazarus to come out. Lazarus, who was dead, came out of the tomb alive, still bound in his burial wrappings.

The gospel of John tells us that many of those who saw this, including the family of Lazarus, came to believe that Jesus was the Son of God because of what they had seen.

They were no longer enslaved by death, but now they had hope in God. They believed that God would deliver them from all their enemies: sin, illness, and even death.

That doesn't make death a pleasant thing in itself, for there is still pain and separation, but it does change our perspective. We still mourn, but no longer like those who live without hope, for we know that death will not triumph over us.

# Nicodemus — The Teacher of Israel

*John 3:1ff; 7:50; 19:38-42*

WHEN a person is poor and weak, it is easy to follow someone who promises deliverance (for there is really very little to lose).

However, when someone is rich, educated, and powerful, it can be much more difficult, for one is risking power and prestige by throwing in one's lot with that deliverer.

Thus, when Jesus began to preach, He was successful with the poor of the Lord, those who were the despised and wretched, but He was largely unsuccessful with the leaders of the land. They had their riches; they didn't need anything else.

There were, of course, exceptions to this pattern, and Nicodemus represents one of those exceptions. He was rich and powerful, one of the teachers of the Jews (and probably a member of the ruling body, the Sanhedrin). He had a lot to lose.

Yet slowly Nicodemus realized that it was all unimportant in comparison to the light that Jesus offered.

Nicodemus' first encounter with Jesus, reported in John 3, was not very promising. John uses Nicodemus as a symbol of the Jews who believed in Jesus, but whose faith was immature.

These Jews still trusted too strongly in their law and their prestige, and they had not yet emptied themselves of their self-sufficiency to place their trust in God.

It is for this reason that Nicodemus came to see Jesus in the middle of the night (he was in the night for he didn't yet know the light, Jesus).

Even though Nicodemus is described as being a teacher of Israel, he keeps misunderstanding what Jesus is telling him. (John shows this by a clever series of wordplays—Jesus says one thing, and Nicodemus understands the other possible meaning.)

Each time that Nicodemus misunderstands, Jesus tries to lead him to a fuller, more profound understanding of what God asks of him. He asks nothing less than that he be reborn in the Spirit.

If people trust in their own power, they are as good as dead. If, however, they trust in the power of God to give new life, they will live forever.

Nicodemus' growth in faith is seen by his two other appearances in the gospel of John. In the first, he subtly defends Jesus in the Sanhedrin; in the other he risks all by providing the oils and spices needed to bury Jesus.

In our prosperous times when it is so easy to place our trust in what we possess or know, Nicodemus calls us to become what he was— one who learned what it was to be reborn in the Spirit by emptying oneself and trusting in God alone.

# Joseph Of Arimathea

*Matthew 27:57; Mark 15:43-46; Luke 23:50-54; John 19:38-42*

NO matter how well we know that something is right, it is often difficult to find the strength to do that thing. On an intellectual level we are without doubt, but we also know the cost if we were to swing into action.

It bothers us that we are being inconsistent, but we are more bothered by the possible consequences of being too consistent—and so, we live with this dilemma until we have no other possibility but to decide for or against.

Joseph of Arimathea seems to have experienced such a dilemma. He was a member of the Sanhedrin, the ruling council of the Jews. He was also a wealthy man.

Like Nicodemus, Joseph had much to lose if he opted to follow Jesus. He would have been ostracized by the other members of the council and possibly worse.

Yet Joseph knew that Jesus was special. He knew that Jesus spoke with the authority of the Spirit of God, and he probably suspected that He was, in fact, the Messiah.

Joseph seems to have opted to play both sides of the fence. Publicly, he was indifferent to Jesus, but secretly he had become one of His disciples (again, not unlike Nicodemus who had visited Jesus at night for fear of the Jews).

By doing this, Joseph showed himself to be a cautious man, one who carefully measured his every move.

The moment arrives in each person's live, though, when we must throw away caution and take a risk. That moment arrived in Joseph's life on the first Good Friday. His master, Jesus, had been arrested, tried, and crucified.

Joseph must have been distraught. All that he had hoped for was no longer possible. Since he was a cautious man, it would have been logical for Joseph to keep his allegiance to this "convicted criminal" a secret. That, however, is not what he did.

Joseph went before Pilate, the Roman governor of Judea, and asked him for permission to take Jesus' body down from the cross. In doing that he exposed himself to the charge of being a coconspirator with Jesus (something from which even Peter fled by denying Jesus three times). He had finally found something (someone) for whom he could live and die.

After he had taken Jesus' body down from the cross, Joseph supplied the spices and linen cloth necessary for a ritual Jewish burial. He also had Jesus placed in his own family tomb. Again, this was an open admission that he belonged to Jesus.

Joseph's life shows us that we are not alone in our hesitancy to live by our principles. We are not the only ones who are inconsistent. It also invites us to take that important step so that we, too, might live and die for the Kingdom.

# Stephen The Church's First Martyr

*Acts 6—7*

SOMETIMES when we think about the early Church, we picture it as being a group of men and women so dedicated to the service of the Lord that there were never any misunderstandings, never any hostility. We read in the Acts of the Apostles, after all, how the early Christians shared all their possessions in common.

This picture of the early Church is not quite accurate. Even within the Acts of the Apostles, there is evidence of tension within the community. There were two ethnic groups among the Jews: those who were of Palestinian origin and those who were from the Diaspora (and who spoke Greek).

The Greek-speaking Jewish Christians felt discriminated against by the Palestinian Jewish Christians. The apostles were all Palestinians, and they controlled the assistance funds which were to aid poor widows and orphans in Jerusalem. The Greek-speakers complained to them that their poor were not receiving as much aid as the Palestinians.

In order to resolve this difficulty, the apostles decided to involve the Greek-speakers in the decision-making process. They invited the Greeks to choose seven of their men who would attend to the task of distributing funds.

Among the men whom they chose was a certain Stephen who is described as being, "a man full of faith and the Holy Spirit." The apostles laid their hands upon these men, thus making them the first deacons of the Church.

It seems as if the duties of these deacons went beyond administering charity within the community. Stephen is pictured as becoming involved with preaching and healing.

A group of Jews became jealous of him because of the great success that he was having in his ministry. They falsely accused him of blaspheming and brought him before the council of the elders.

It was before that council that Stephen gave his greatest witness to the faith. In a long speech he outlined the history of the Jewish people, showing all the wonders that God had done for them and how they had still rebelled against Him.

At the end of the speech, Stephen's face became transformed, for he saw Jesus standing at the right hand of God. When he proclaimed this, the Jews were enraged for he was stating that Jesus was equal to the Father (which, for them, was a blasphemy).

They dragged him out of the city and stoned him to death. Saul (also known as Paul) is said to have participated in this infamous act.

Stephen was thus the first martyr of the early Church (martyr means nothing else than witness, for he testified before all of God's love to us through Jesus). His courage challenges us to live and proclaim our faith fearlessly, no matter what the cost.

# Philip The Deacon

*Acts 6:5; 8; 21:8f*

WHEN we face adversity in our lives, one of our first reactions is often to accuse God of abandoning us. We cannot understand how He would allow these evil things to happen to someone who is trying to follow His call.

We do not trust in God enough to believe that He will work all things to the good (even things which seem to be terribly negative).

The story of Philip the Deacon should be a lesson for us. Philip was one of the seven Greek-speaking men chosen by the apostles to take care of the charitable activities of the early Church. The apostles designated these men as deacons by imposing hands on them, thus sharing with them the power of the Lord.

The activities of the deacons were not always greeted favorably. Shortly after their call, one of their number, Stephen, was martyred. Following that disaster, a great persecution broke out against the Church, and all of the rest of the deacons were forced to flee from Jerusalem. (It seems as if the persecution was directed against the Greek-speaking Jewish Christians and not the Palestinian Jewish Christians.)

Philip, one of those fleeing, could easily have been discouraged by these events. Rather, he saw them as a possibility to do the work of God. He began to preach to the Samaritan villages to which he fled.

The Samaritans were a group of Jews who did not follow all of the laws of the Jews in Jerusalem. They were considered to be heretics by the main-line Jews.

When Philip began to preach to them, he was extending the message of the Lord beyond the traditional Jews to a group that we could call "half-Jews." He met with great success in this apostolic activity.

The Spirit of the Lord soon directed him to go beyond this group to people who were not even Jews (but who were at least sympathetic to the Jewish religion). An Ethiopian official was returning to his homeland from Jerusalem. He was reading the book of the prophet Isaiah as he was being carried along on his litter, but he could not understand it fully.

Philip explained to him that the things written in that prophecy had to do with Jesus. He then baptized the Ethiopian.

Through Philip's activity, the new faith spread from a traditional base in Jerusalem to encompass those who were not quite normal Jews. It was the first step in the process of extending the message to the pagans.

Rather then letting adversity hinder the message, Philip had used it as an occasion to do God's will. This is something that we might learn from him and try to apply in our lives.

# Paul The Missionary

*Acts; Letters of Paul*

MOST of us come to know God in a gradual manner. If we grow up in a religious family, we learn about Him as we learn all our other lessons.

There are some, though, who meet God in a radical conversion. Life suddenly makes no sense except in the context of God.

Paul of Tarsus is one of those who met God in a most radical manner. It is not that he wasn't a religious man, for he was that from his youth. One might even say that he was exemplary for he strove to observe the law perfectly.

The only problem was that although he was highly religious, he really didn't know God. He was serving theories and law and not God Himself. Since the new sect of Christians was opposing the traditional religious beliefs, he combated them with all his force. They were dangerous for they opposed religion as he knew it.

Then one day while on the road to Damascus he had a vision. It was a vision of Christ asking Paul why he was persecuting Him. In that vision Paul met Christ as a person, and it completely changed his life.

Paul saw that the law was relative and practices were relative as opposed to the eternal truth found in Jesus. He served that truth with his every breath from that day on.

It was about the time that Paul was converted that the Church had to make a crucial decision. Its leaders had to decide whether they should continue to evangelize the Jews alone or whether they should go out to the pagans as well.

Paul, who before his conversion was enslaved to tradition, saw this as a tremendous opportunity to spread the word of God. He spearheaded the drive to convert the pagans to Christ.

Paul defended the rights of these newly converted Christians by arguing that, since they were freed from sin by faith in Jesus, there was no reason why they should have to follow Jewish law.

Paul traveled from city to city preaching the Good News to anyone who would listen to him. He would first go to the synagogues in each city, but if they would not listen to him, he would turn to the pagans.

Eventually Paul had built up an entire system of Christian communities. These communities had serious doubts concerning how they should follow Christ (there was no real hierarchy yet to guide them nor were the Gospels even written yet).

Since he couldn't be everywhere at once, Paul wrote the Churches to instruct them, exhort them, comfort them, and sometimes just to express his love and concern for them.

Paul gave his all to those whom he served. He suffered much in his missionary journeys, for he was robbed, stoned, lashed, shipwrecked. Eventually he even gave up his life in martyrdom in Rome for the sake of the God whom he knew and loved.

# Barnabas The Courageous Disciple

*Acts 4:36; 9:27; 11:22ff; 13:1ff; 14:8ff; 15:1ff; Galatians 2:13; 1 Corinthians 9:6*

IT is often advisable to be cautious in charting new frontiers, but it can also be stifling if someone tries to be too cautious. Every once in a while we need someone who will be courageous enough to set a course into the unknown, risking all for the sake of the cause.

Barnabas was one of those individuals. A Jew from Cyprus, he is first mentioned in the Acts of the Apostles (4:36) where he is said to have sold his property and given the money from its sale to the apostles. The fact that he did this already points to a generous disposition—one ready to take risks.

Barnabas was soon called upon to take even greater risks. Paul, who had only recently converted to the Lord on the road to Damascus, arrived in Jerusalem and asked to meet with the apostles. The apostles were hesitant to accede to his request, for Paul had been famous for his attacks on the Church.

Barnabas was courageous, though, and he arranged to have Paul introduced to the apostles—a momentous event in the history of the Church.

When word came to Jerusalem that the word of the Lord was being preached to Greek pagans in the city of Antioch, the apostles were once again skeptical. This had never been done before. They sent Barnabas to that city to investigate.

Barnabas' response was to rejoice greatly at what he found. He was not worried about the newness of the pagan mission, but rather celebrated the fact that the word of the Lord was not restricted to the Jews alone. He sent for Paul to assist him in ministering to the needs of this nascent community.

Barnabas and Paul also engaged in missionary activities. They were called by their community in Antioch to serve the Lord by preaching the Gospel. Taking Mark along, they sailed to Cyprus and Asia Minor and were quite successful.

The mission was so successful, in fact, that the question arose as to whether pagan Christians should be obliged to observe Judaic law. Barnabas went with Paul to Jerusalem and met with the apostles.

The conclusion of the meeting was that no new burdens should be laid upon the pagans other than avoiding immorality and not eating meat that had been offered to idols. Barnabas would not allow tradition to stifle the Good News.

Barnabas did have one disagreement with Paul. Mark, a cousin of Barnabas, had accompanied him and Paul on a missionary journey. For some reason he left them, an act that greatly upset Paul.

When Paul and Barnabas prepared to leave on their next journey, they argued over whether Mark should be allowed to accompany them, and they each went their separate ways. The rift seems to have healed, though, for Paul later wrote of Barnabas in complimentary terms.

# Mark The Evangelist

*Mark 14:51-52; Acts 12:12ff; 15:37; Colossians 4:10; Philemon 24; 2 Timothy 4:11; 1 Peter 5:13*

WHEN we hear important news, we often want to share it with others. We will run off and tell it to our family and friends, and possibly even phone or write someone who lives at a distance.

The need to share the news increases proportionally with its importance, so that a monumental event might even spark the idea of sharing the event with future generations by preserving a written account.

Mark (or John Mark, as he is called in the Acts of the Apostles) realized that the event to which he was giving witness was the central event in the history of humanity. His need to share the Good News caused him to write the Gospel that bears his name, the first of the Gospels to be written.

We first meet Mark in the Acts of the Apostles. He accompanied Paul and Barnabas, his cousin, on a missionary trip to Cyprus and Asia Minor.

For some reason, Mark left his companions and returned to Jerusalem (an action that terribly annoyed Paul and even caused friction between Paul and Barnabas). Whatever the difficulty, it seems that it was eventually settled, for Paul wrote favorably of Mark in his letter to Philemon.

Having grown up in Jerusalem, Mark may have known Jesus in the flesh (many believe that he is the young boy mentioned in the Garden of Gethsemani on the night when Jesus was arrested). Yet most of the information for his gospel seems to have been acquired from others.

Mark was a companion of Peter, and much of what he wrote is said to have been handed down to Mark by the prince of the apostles. Mark probably also drew upon the various written accounts of miracles and events in the life of Jesus that were around in his time.

When Mark finally decided to prepare a written version of his Good News, he seems to have done it with a specific goal and audience in mind. It is believed that Mark wrote for a Gentile audience. Not being Jews, they were unfamiliar with many of the phrases and customs that a Jewish audience would take for granted.

Mark went out of his way to explain these difficult ideas to them. He presented his audience with a very straightforward picture of Jesus. He wanted to show the pagans that Jesus was really a man and not a myth like their gods.

In his early career, Mark's future did not appear bright. Yet he accomplished great things in writing his gospel.

This turn of events is a warning to us not to categorize people, but to allow them to use their creativity in serving God. This often requires patience while individuals search for their own way, but only in this manner will the real Good News be preached.

# Luke   The Divine Physician

*Colossians 4:14; 2 Timothy 4:11; Philemon 24; Acts 13:1; Romans 16:21*

WHEN people write a book, they tend to put a lot of themselves into that work. Those things which they consider to be important can be seen by the way certain things are emphasized while others are relegated to a less prominent position.

This is true even of biographies. Biographers never give a totally objective picture of their subject, and they often betray more of their own concerns than they realize.

The evangelists are no exceptions to this observation. Each of the evangelists wrote for a particular audience and with certain aims in mind. Even more, their own personal vision of what is truly important entered into their accounts.

Luke, for example, was a doctor. He dedicated himself to the service of the weak and the ill: those in need of his loving concern. He joined Paul in his missionary journeys because he saw that humanity was desperately in need of spiritual healing and the Good News that he received was the instrument of that healing.

After Paul's death, Luke recognized that he was being called to a different form of the apostolate. The Church was entering its second generation. The new converts were mostly pagans who knew little about the early days of the Church. Luke decided to write a history of Christ's ministry and the spread of that Good News after the resurrection.

Luke's account was more than simply informational, for it also wished to show that Jesus intended for the Church to develop as it had. While the message was first addressed to the Jews, it was intended to go to the pagans (as is seen in the Acts of the Apostles).

This was the primary aim of Luke's gospel and the Acts, but it does not exhaust the richness of his message. Something of Luke's concern for the poor and downtrodden is seen all throughout his account.

Luke shows the family of Jesus (Mary, Elizabeth, Zechariah) to be among the poor ones of Yahweh. Jesus, a poor one born among the poor, brings the message of salvation to those without hope.

Many of the parables and stories that appear only in the gospel of Luke emphasize this theme. His gospel speaks of Lazarus and the rich man, of the need to invite the poor to a banquet, of the need for total renunciation among the followers of Jesus. His gospel also shows Jesus reaching out to the spiritually poor: the prodigal son, the lost drachma.

Luke certainly did not betray Christ's message by emphasizing these things over others. Rather, his unique view of life gained while he was a doctor allowed him to see that Christ was indeed the doctor of those without hope.

# Timothy The Leader in the Lord

*Acts 16:1-3; 17:14f; 19:22; 20:4; Letters of Paul; 1 and 2 Timothy*

WHEN people who judge with the standards of the world gain power, their priorities are often to enjoy that power and to preserve it at all costs. They are concerned with their own interests, and power is the means to defend those interests.

It is different when one who serves Christ is put in charge of a community. That person must live for the community and use power to serve (and not to be served).

Even though we know this to be true, it is not always easy to live accordingly. In the days of Christ, for example, there were few examples of what we could call a Christian use of authority.

The models of authority in those days were the officials of the empire: the emperor, kings, governors. Very rarely were they concerned with the interests of their subjects. Most often they did just what was necessary so that rebellion would not occur (and no more).

Within the Jewish world things were not really any better. The Kings of the Jews ruled as oriental potentates and absolute monarchs. The religious leaders of the Jews lorded it over their subjects.

It was for this reason that Jesus took care to teach His apostles how to be servants of all. Likewise, when Paul appointed men to be the religious leaders of communities, he instructed them carefully on the duties of a leader in Christ.

The two letters of Timothy are part of this type of an instruction. It seems that the letters were not actually written by Paul, but they do reflect Paul's concern for this issue as seen in his authentic writings.

Timothy was a companion of Paul during his missionary journeys. He was the son of a mixed marriage (pagan father and Jewish mother). Since one is Jewish if one's mother is Jewish, Paul allowed for him to be circumcised when Timothy turned to Christ.

Timothy proved to be an important asset to Paul's activities for when Paul could not be in an area where a missionary was needed, he would send Timothy to represent him (e.g., Thessalonica).

The letters to Timothy are concerned with how Timothy should lead the community at Ephesus.

Timothy was to be fearless in defending the truth and exposing lies. He was to be a source of unity to the community, but not at the cost of allowing factions to exist. He was to lead an exemplary life, controling himself to avoid any type of excess.

Timothy was to take special care that the worship of the community was conducted in a proper manner. Most of all, he was to follow Paul's example of pouring out his life for those whom he was to serve. This is the pattern for all true Christian leaders.

# Titus  One of the First Bishops

*Galatians 2:1ff; 2 Corinthians; 2 Timothy 4:10; Titus*

WITH every new organization of almost any type, there are various stages of development. Very often it is formed by one person who is a charismatic leader. He or she draws others, and slowly the organization takes shape.

When that person passes from the scene, there is a moment of crisis. Either the organization falls apart because it cannot exist without its founder or it begins to become institutionalized. By becoming an institution, the organization makes up what is lacking when its founder (who led by charism rather than law) is no longer there.

This pattern which is true of most organizations can be seen in the early Church as well. While Jesus was on earth, there was no real need for a formalized organization. When He ascended into heaven, some type of hierarchy was needed to continue to spread His message.

Although the organization seems to have been very loose, it is nevertheless true that the apostles were leaders in the Church. Even beyond that, some of the apostles seem to have been part of a ruling body, for Paul calls them the pillars of the Church (Peter, James, and John).

When that first generation of the Church began to pass away, there was desperate need for more organization. The apostles and missionaries began to appoint leaders for each of the communities.

These were the first real bishops and presbyters (elders) of the Church. It was in that generation that we find Timothy and Titus.

Titus was a disciple of Paul. He accompanied Paul to Jerusalem, and he also served as his emissary to the community in Corinth.

The Corinthian community was torn apart by divisions and strife. Titus was able to bring them together and help them make peace with Paul (with whom they had been feuding). Paul greatly appreciated his holy work.

The letter to Titus (which, like the letters to Timothy, was attributed to Paul but was probably not written by him) posits that Titus was a bishop in Crete. According to this letter, he had been sent there by Paul to help discipline the Church and to establish a dependable local hierarchy.

"Paul" tells him how a bishop and his family should act. He also warns him about those who would pervert the truth (he calls them the "circumcision party"—they are probably those who would want Christians to follow Jewish laws).

Even if this letter was not written by Paul, it is valuable for it reflects what was going on in the Church. Men like Titus were being asked to save the Church by assuming authority so that the work of the Lord could prosper.

# WORD LIST

**Anawim "The poor of Yahweh."** These were the lowly and humble people of Israel who relied totally upon the Lord and not upon their own strength.

**Anoint.** To apply oil to someone as part of a sacred rite—as a sign of honor or appointment to some special work. The king in Israel was anointed upon taking office and was known as the anointed one. This became the title of the Messianic King, since Messiah means "anointed."

**Apocalyptic** A type of writing that spoke of an end to the present era and the beginning of a new, perfect era. It is characterized by visions, dreams, and much symbolism.

**Apostles.** Twelve men chosen by Christ to enjoy special jurisdiction and to teach. They are Peter, John, James, Andrew, Philip, Thomas, Bartholomew, Matthew, James the Lesser, Simon the Zealot, Jude, and Judas, who was replaced by Matthias. Paul and Barnabas are also called Apostles, which means literally "one who is sent."

**Baal.** The god of the pagan inhabitants of Canaan, a god of fertility and rain.

**Babylon.** Capital of Babylonia, to which many Jewish captives were deported after the fall of Jerusalem in 587 B.C.; this is known as the Babylonian Captivity or the Exile.

**Ban.** The law of Moses in accord with the customs of the time, called for the practice of a "ban." This could be applied to animals for sacrifice, to property given to God, or even to any person or persons found worthy of death. These were said to be "doomed" or "devoted to the Lord," and they could not be used by humans.

**Canaan.** A name for the territory of Israel. Its original inhabitants (pagans) were called Canaanites.

**Christ.** A name (from the Greek) given to the Incarnate Word meaning "The Anointed One" or "The Messiah." This was His official title and revealed to the Jews that He was the King and Redeemer they awaited. Jesus, which means "the Lord is salvation" or "Savior," is His personal name and denotes His mission: to save people from death and sin; make them once more children of God and heirs of heaven.

**Circumcision.** A religious rite chosen by God to be the external sign of the Covenant God made with Abraham and all his descendants. In the New Covenant, it is replaced by baptism which marks with a spiritual and indelible sign Christians who are *spiritual* descendants of Abraham.

**Covenant.** A pact between two parties. In the Bible, it refers especially to the promise of God to Israel that He would be their God and they would be His people.

**Diaspora.** Jews who no longer lived in Israel (either through exile or migration). In Jesus' day, most Diaspora Jews spoke Greek as a first language.

**Disciple.** A person who follows a prophet, a teacher, etc., is instructed by him, and becomes a follower of his teaching.

**Dreams.** The Bible forbids attaching importance to dreams. However, they are sometimes presented as a means employed by God for making His will known.

**Essenes.** A group of monks who lived on the shores of the Dead Sea and who led pure lives awaiting the coming of a priestly and/or kingly Messiah.

**Figure.** A person, event, or object which in God's intention signifies or foreshadows something else. Many realities of the Old Testament foreshadowed those of the New.

**Gospel.** The Good News of salvation brought to the world by Jesus Christ and recorded in the New Testament.

**High Priest.** The head of the Jewish priestly system. He offered sacrifice daily and entered once a year into the Holy of Holies to offer sacrifice for himself and the people. As head of the Sanhedrin, he wielded great political influence.

**Israel.** Either all of the Jewish Kingdom or the northern kingdom (after the reign of Solomon).

**Judah.** The southern kingdom of the Jews (after the reign of Solomon).

**Judges.** Charismatic leaders of Israel. They were warlords, administrators of justice, and viceroys of the king of Israel, Yahweh. The judges led Israel from the conquest of Joshua until the advent of the first king, Saul.

**Kingdom of God.** In the Old Testament the Kingdom of God represents: (1) the universal rule of God over all creatures, (2) the Hebrew nation, (3) the Messianic Kingdom to be instituted by the Messiah. In the New Testament, this Kingdom is described as having been established by Jesus and pertains to the present and *future* (it will be consummated in heaven).

**Law of Moses.** The law, respected by all Jews as from God, consisted of the five books of Moses. These formed the basis of the Scripture reading and instruction in the synagogue services. In addition the Pharisees observed a traditional law, the *Mishna,* which they taught also had its author in Moses. Jesus observed the Mosaic law and promulgated for His followers its basic element, the Ten Commandments. He criticized the Pharisees for their neglect of it in favor of their traditions.

**Messiah.** A Hebrew word signifying to be consecrated priest or king by an anointing. The Greek word corresponding to this is Christ (see **Christ**).

**Passover.** Feast instituted to commemorate the Departure from Egypt with the "passing over" of the Angel of death and the crossing of the Reed Sea. Each Israelite family (as their ancestors had done) immolated a lamb and ate it, following a minutely described rite with unleavened bread and bitter herbs. At this observance Jesus instituted the Holy Eucharist.

**Pharisees.** Jewish sect which sought the perfect expression of spiritual life through strict observance of the Law and tradition alone.

**Philistines.** Non-Semitic invaders who gave their name to Palestine although they occupied only its south-western plains.

**Priestly School.** A school of writers who wrote during the exile in Babylon (after 587 B.C.). They were concerned with laws and cultic material.

**Prophets.** Men (and some women) chosen by God to speak in His name. They were the teachers and guardians of the religion of Israel, advisers to kings, defenders of the poor and oppressed, and heralds of the Messiah and His Kingdom.

**Sadducees.** A nationalistic Jewish sect. They believed in God but rejected the oral traditions of their forefathers.

**Samaritans.** A sect of "heretical" Jews. They were descendents of the Jews left in the northern kingdom after the Assyrian exile who had intermarried with foreigners. They accepted only the first five books of the Bible as valid.

**Sanhedrin.** The ruling council of the Jews during the time of Jesus. It was composed of Pharisees and Sadducees and decided religious questions for the nation (the Romans decided other issues).

**Scriptures.** (1) The inspired books, the work of the Holy Spirit. They were customarily divided into three series: the Law, the Prophets, and the Writings. (2) Christianity added its own writings: the Gospels and the Letters of the Apostles.

**Seleucid.** The Syrian empire founded by Seleucus, a general of Alexander the Great. Under Antiochus Epiphanes, one of the Seleucid emperors, a great persecution broke out against the Jews.

**Son of Man.** A Messianic title found in the Prophet Daniel and used by Jesus, who by means of it progressively revealed Himself as the Messiah to the Jews.

**Synagogue.** A place where the Jews gathered on the Sabbath to listen to the explanations of the Bible. Each locality had one in place of the temple of Jerusalem.

**Synoptic Gospels.** The gospels of Matthew, Mark, and Luke, so called because these three gospels are quite similar when compared to the gospel of John.

**Temple.** House of worship which was built by Solomon, destroyed and then rebuilt after the Babylonian Captivity, and finally destroyed in 70 A.D., by the Romans.

**Yahweh.** The personal name of God given to Moses from the burning bush. The name is so sacred that only the high priest could pronounce it, and even he could only do that once a year.

**Yahwist School.** A school of writers in the court of kings David and Solomon, c. 950 B.C. These are the first writers to write large sections of the Bible. They are characterized by their use of the name of Yahweh when they refer to God.

**Zealots.** A party of nationalistic Jews who opposed Roman rule in Israel, often through violent means.

# INDEX
Boldface numerals indicate where main entries are treated.

# OTHER OUTSTANDING CATHOLIC BOOKS